The Essential Daily Planner for Real Estate Agents

THE ESSENTIAL DAILY PLANNER FOR REAL ESTATE AGENTS

Success in 10 Minutes a Day

Melissa Zavala

MELROSE PUBLICATIONS
San Diego
2013

"Only those who will risk going too far can possibly find out
how far one can go."

—T.S. Eliot

The topic of real estate agent business planning is not unique, and much of the information in this planner is common knowledge. The following sources were consulted when creating the lists and charts on pages 14–15 and pages 230–235: *Shift: How Top Agents Tackle Tough Times* (Gary Keller), *The Real Estate Agent's Business Planning Guide* (Carla Cross), and *2011 Real Estate Business Plan* (Market Leader).

www.melrosepublications.com

ISBN 978-0-9860526-1-3
Printed in the United States of America

Cover by Marquardt Design

CONTENTS

INTRODUCTION

When recently cleaning out my desk, I dredged up a drawer full of random pieces of paper with sloppy handwritten notes all over them. What a mess! One sticky note contained a name and a phone number next to the words "send out email campaigns." Another had a list of office supplies that I needed to purchase.

I'm not proud that I have a penchant for jotting things down on the first piece of paper that I find. In fact, if I am in the midst of a conversation and don't have my planner with me, I still make random notes on whatever piece of paper is closest to me.

I've got to say that after a few years in real estate, I began to notice a pattern—and it wasn't a very good one. After calling my assistant for about the 23rd time to request that she attempt to locate a yellow or pink piece of paper that I may have left on my desk and which contained a very important name or phone number, I decided that something needed to change. My thoughts were scattered, and my notes were scattered; I felt that I lacked focus. I needed to keep track of everything in one place—a book that I could carry around with me all the time.

Using a daily planner to keep track of your real estate activities is invaluable in more ways than you may imagine. Not only is a planner a great place to make notes and set appointments, but it is also a wonderful organizational tool. *The Essential Daily Planner for Real Estate Agents* is structured to help real estate agents set worthy goals and plan strategies to achieve them. Additionally, the educational tips and the organizational tools contained within the pages will encourage you to stick to your business plan, and bring you a sense of accomplishment. It doesn't matter whether you are a new agent or a top producer with decades of experience, whether you are aiming to sell ten homes or one thousand, your planner will get you results.

Imagine going on a trip with no particular destination. How would you pack? Which roads would you take? How would you know that you have arrived? Generally, when you plan a trip, you select your destination. The same is true for the goals or milestones in your life. Writing down your goals compels you to consider your destination; you decide what you want.

There's something magical that happens when you take time to document your goals and objectives. The physical act of committing your goals to writing will force you to clarify what you want and overcome resistance at the same time. Further, it will enable you to see—and celebrate—your progress.

Life is hard. It is particularly difficult when you aren't seeing progress. You feel like you are working hard, but going nowhere. Written goals, especially micro-goals or process-oriented goals, are like mile markers on a highway. They enable you to see how far you have come and how far you need to go. Process-oriented goals also provide an opportunity for immediate celebration when you achieve them.

Of course, sometimes we try too hard, running ourselves ragged, and in those instances, your daily planner will come in handy, too. Tracking your daily real estate activities—your calls, your prospecting, your marketing, your networking, and your professional development— is the best way to evaluate your processes.

When you track your daily real estate activities for days, weeks, and months, patterns emerge. Your planner will reveal the strategies that work well for you, and those that leave you feeling disappointed and uninspired. You will note certain activities that were more successful, and those that appear to be a waste of time or money. Only then can you reassess or redirect your energy towards the accomplishments that make you successful.

It's so easy to forget what you did two days ago, let alone two weeks ago. Without records, you might perceive that you're only doing a certain activity two days a week when you may actually be doing it more. A planner keeps you honest and holds you account-able when you veer off course. It helps you to believe in yourself, reminding you of all of the activities you have completed, the effort you've expended, and the progress you've made.

In *The Essential Daily Planner for Real Estate Agents,* you'll track your daily activities as well as your goals for each week and for the next six months. You'll even find tools to help you chart a course to success in the field of real estate. According to author, real estate investor, and co-founder of Keller Williams Realty, Gary Keller, "If we know where we're going and what we want to accomplish, this gives us amazing clarity on our priority." When you know what you want to achieve and you document the stepping stones along the way to your objectives, your goals will be exceedingly clear. It is my hope that in using this planner for just 10 minutes a day, you will achieve great success in the field of real estate.

SETTING GOALS

Famous Major League Baseball catcher, outfielder, and manager, Yogi Berra once said, "If you don't know where you are going, you might wind up someplace else." Known for his quips called Yogi-isms, Berra makes a good point. The best way to achieve your goals is to set them—to know where you are going.

The mark of a successful real estate agent is the ability to set goals and create action plans in order to accomplish those goals. It's sometimes hard to find the time to actually sit down and consider your personal and business goals. However, the single activity of writing down and assessing your objectives will greatly impact what you can achieve in the field of real estate and beyond. Goal setting requires two types of discipline: 1) the discipline to sit down and make a list of all of the things you want to accomplish, and 2) the ability to consistently work a plan that will enable you to achieve your goals.

With goal setting often comes disappointment, since setting goals is not a perfect science. Due to changes that may occur in the economy or in your personal life, some goals may need to be altered or revised throughout the year.

The Essential Daily Planner for Real Estate Agents is designed and organized in order to assist you in both recording your business goals and motivating you to achieve them. The following ten tips will help you as you create and reflect on your personal and professional goals.

Ten Tips for Setting Personal and Professional Goals

1. Goals Must Be Specific, Detailed, and Clear.

You must invest the time to put your goals in written form. There is a direct connection between writing a goal, seeing it written, and having it become embedded in your subconscious mind. The goals you set must be specific, not vague. To say that you want to be "rich" or "successful" is not specific enough. Your goal must be both realistic and concrete. Concise and well-defined goals are achieved, and ambiguous goals are forgotten.

> **Goal:** To sell a lot homes
> **Better Goal:** To sell <u>12</u> homes

2. Goals Must Be Measurable.

It's hard to quantify happiness and success, since the definition of each of those feelings is different for everyone. For this very reason, every real estate agent must be able to analyze and evaluate progress and results in a tangible way. Many people have a goal of becoming rich. Since rich is not quantifiable, it would be better to provide a measurable definition of rich. It's always easier to evaluate whether a goal has been accomplished when it is a measurable one.

> **Goal:** To sell 12 homes
> **Better Goal:** To sell 12 homes and <u>earn $60,000 in net commission</u>

3. Goals Have Deadlines.

The best goals always have a date by which they need to be accomplished. Additionally, they have interim steps along the way that can be monitored. These sub-deadlines or micro-objectives are the stepping stones to success. Remember that there are no unrealistic goals, but there can be unrealistic deadlines.

> **Goal:** To sell 12 homes and earn $60,000 in net commission
> **Better Goal:** To sell 12 homes <u>in 6 months</u> and earn $60,000 in net commission

4. Goals Should Be Challenging Yet Realistic.

Some people are motivated by goals that are far out of reach, and others give up if they are not even close to meeting their goals. It's a good idea to set realistic goals based on what you know about what you can do and what you have done in the past. For example, if you know that you sold 4 homes per month last year, it would not be unrealistic to set a goal to sell 5 homes per month this year.

A realistic goal that is slightly out of reach will push you to the next level. Ralph Waldo Emerson is famous for saying "Life is a journey, not a destination." Even if you do not meet your exact goal (perhaps closing 10 transactions, instead of 12), the process of working towards that goal has taught you some things that will assist you in meeting future goals. Your real estate career is a journey, and not a destination. Everything you do will teach you how to better achieve your goals in the future.

5. Not All Goals Are Long Term.

There are two sets of objectives that you need to set in order to achieve: the short-term ones and the long-term ones. The short-term goals drive what you do each and every day, and the long-term goals drive the planning for larger term efforts surrounding what you want to achieve.

Long-term goals, such as closing 100 transactions in five years or running your first marathon in 18 months, will flood your brain. However, you will need to establish interim steps in order to achieve those goals. Smaller, more immediate goals will keep you on track and make your dreams achievable. Set interim goals that outline what needs to be accomplished every six or eight weeks; you can also set daily and weekly goals. Setting an intention for each and every day will lead to success in achieving your long-term goals.

6. Focus on a Few Goals.

Don't set too many targets. Most of us strive to make more sales and obtain more leads. In order to accomplish those goals, you need persistence and self-discipline. Anyone that tries to accomplish too many objectives (such as selecting too many target markets or attempting too many activities in one week) will probably become frustrated and see more limited success. Assess your priorities and focus on reaching the goals that are most important to you right now.

7. Focus on Process Rather than Outcome Goals.

Concentrate on the things that you can control (the processes) instead of those that you cannot (the outcomes). For example, you may not be able to control how many transactions actually close, but you can control how many prospects you contact, how often you post on social media sites, and how often you send out an email campaign to your circle of influence.

Always set measurable objectives that you can control. Work to connect these measurable objectives to specific outcomes.

> **Process Goal:** Deliver 3 Expired Listing Packages per Week
> **Outcome Goal:** Convert 1 Expired Listing Package Delivery into 1 Listing per Month

Succeeding at your objectives (your "process" goals) will boost your morale if life gets in the way of achieving your long-term goals.

8. Develop Strategies to Achieve Your Goals.

Setting goals isn't worth much without a plan to get you to your destination. Just as a triathlete may need to work with a trainer in order to prepare for the next race, you may need to work with your Broker, a Mastermind partner, or a real estate coach in order to devise a business plan or hone your current one. To get started, review the materials on pages 230–236 of this book. These items are available to help you to set both long-term and short-term goals.

Even the simplest goals require strategizing. For example, if you aim to close two deals per month, examine the obstacles that have hindered you in the past and make some changes. Maybe you need to get some additional technology training in order to market to a new generation of homebuyers. Perhaps you need to wake up 30 minutes earlier in order to regularly attend your local Realtor® marketing session. Develop new strategies and revisit old ones in order to continually achieve success in a changing real estate market.

9. Goals Must Align with Your Ethics.

Your goals need to align with your personal values and beliefs. Your goals also have to be harmonious with each other. For example, let's say that you want to lose 10 pounds. However, you also want to eat a gallon of ice cream every night before you go to sleep. One of these two things will need to give way to the other. They are not harmonious. There is no way you can achieve both at the same time. You cannot achieve goals that are contrary to one another, and you should not set goals that breach your personal code of ethics.

10. Goals Cannot Be All Business.

Your goals must span all aspects of your life—not just your professional accomplishments. Include personal, social, financial, spiritual, and even physical objectives. Just as a wheel needs balance to rotate properly; we need balance to get anywhere in life. If you spend all day and night meeting your business goals, you may put your personal relationships in jeopardy. Ironically, it is probably those very relationships that are the basis for setting those business goals in the first place!

Life Happens

Goals are a great place to start, but life happens. There are things that occur that are beyond your control and may cause you to reevaluate your goals or the ways in which you plan to achieve your goals. If things do not go according to plan, cut yourself some slack. It's admirable that you completed your processes. However, now you may need to alter those processes and develop a revised daily plan.

MAKING ENTRIES IN YOUR PLANNER

It's a misnomer. We do not manage time. We manage activities. The root of a real estate agent's time management problems lies in a misunderstanding of the job description; that is, agents do not know exactly which activities they should accomplish in order to earn a commission check. With *The Essential Daily Planner for Real Estate Agents*, a real estate agent can stay on track and achieve success in just 10 minutes a day!

Here's the bottom line: A real estate salesperson finds prospects that want to purchase homes. He or she qualifies the prospects, shows properties, and sells homes. A real estate salesperson also finds prospects that want to sell their homes. He or she qualifies prospects, lists and sells clients' homes.

Notice that people—that is, buyers and sellers—are intrinsic to the activities that real estate salespeople need to succeed. It is interesting to note, however, that many of the activities that agents complete during their business day do not involve people who will buy or sell with the agent. Instead, the daily tasks involve things—seeing homes, conducting market analyses, following up, completing paperwork, and attending meetings and classes. When a real estate agent's daily activities get top heavy with things, the agent is set up for failure.

One of the major tenets of a well-developed business plan is a cycle of activities that includes more people than things. When you actively use all of the components of *The Essential Daily Planner for Real Estate Agents*, you are encouraged to put people before things.

It's Your Planner

This is your daily planner; you can make notes all over it or you can leave lots of blank spaces. Some people thrive on details, and others focus on broad strokes. The amount of information that you track every day will vary based upon your mood and your goals.

Even if you only record minimal information, note something every day—including the days that you do not do anything real-estate related. That way, when you look back, you'll be able to distinguish between the times that you took the day off and the days when you avoided writing in your daily planner. If you find yourself having too many days without real estate activities, ask yourself why. Have you lost your passion for real estate? Is something else in your life getting in the way of meeting your objectives?

The following tips are provided to help you fill out each section of your daily planner. Many agents may already have their own systems, but the suggestions on the following pages provide support for novice and experienced agents looking to see increased success in only 10 minutes a day.

Your Goals for the Next Six Months

When you complete the Goal Setting Chart on page 236, you have the opportunity to consider the big picture: your current real estate objectives and processes, and what you would like to accomplish over the next 26 weeks. You'll find a sample on the next page.

Six months is the perfect amount of time for setting long-term goals: it's close enough to make your goals feel attainable, yet far enough into the future to allow for making major progress. At the end of the 26 weeks, review the chart you created on page 236, and see how your results have matched up with your goals. You'll be excited to see how far you have come.

In the Overall Goals section, note your income and production goals. Whatever your aspirations, fill in the Starting Point section for each category—recording details about your current processes and successes. Fill in the Goals space where appropriate. You may find it overwhelming to set goals in all categories at once. And, in some categories, setting precise goals may not be practical—especially if you are new to the field of real estate.

GOALS for the next 6 months

OVERALL GOALS
Earnings: _____ $60,000 _____
Deals Closed: _____ 12 _____

PROSPECTING GOALS
Starting Point: Contact 25 people in my circle of influence twice a month by phone

Goals: Hold 3 open houses per month, contact local FSBOs daily

MARKETING GOALS
Starting Point: Website

Goals: Just Listed/Just Sold Cards, create a blog and facebook business page

NETWORKING GOALS
Starting Point: Attend local marketing sessions once a month

Goals: Attend marketing sessions weekly, join local Chamber of Commerce

PROFESSIONAL DEVELOPMENT GOALS
Starting Point: Attend two classes at my brokerage per month

Goals: Watch three webinars per month, read one real estate or sales book every six weeks

	NUMBER OF CLOSINGS	AVERAGE COMMISSION PER CLOSING
Last 6 Months	8	$38,000
Goal for Next 6 Months	12	$60,000

Using the Daily Planner

The following ideas can be used to fill in each section of your daily planner.

How to Complete the Daily Pages

Weekly Goals: Remember that one of the ten tips for successful goal setting is to focus on process objectives rather than outcomes. While your six-month goal may be a specific number of deals closed or a certain amount of earned commission, the weekly goals that are written at the top of the Monday pages should focus on smaller outcomes or processes.

Though it's important to select concrete objectives, keep in mind that not all of the best goals involve numbers. You might aim to become more skilled at creating Craigslist ads or more proficient at objection handling. Whatever your goal, make sure that you involve people as opposed to things—since it is your relationships with others that will lead to increased closings.

Daily Tip: At the top of almost every page of *The Essential Daily Planner for Real Estate Agents* is a daily motivator. These are customized messages of encouragement and tools for professional development. They include tips in the areas of professional development, networking, marketing, technology, and prospecting. And, if you are looking for some new real estate activity to jumpstart a run-of-the-mill day, then you should look no further. The 130 real estate tips and the 26 motivational quotes provide you with plenty of ways to put your business plan in high gear.

Daily Goals: Daily goals or tasks are where you drill down to the everyday processes that must be completed to achieve your outcomes—your bigger goals. These are outlined further in the Prospecting Tasks and Marketing Tasks sections on the next page. Once you develop a routine for success, you may find that it is a good idea to always do certain things on specific days of the week. For example, you may want to mail postcards on Mondays. This level of consistency is one of the marks of a successful agent.

Prospecting Tasks: Use this section in order to record prospecting tasks or processes that you aim to achieve on a given day. As a real estate agent, your goal is lead generation. Lead generation falls into two categories: prospecting and marketing. You are prospecting when you actively obtain the leads yourself. You are marketing when you do things that make the leads come to you. It's you making contact with people as opposed to *people* making contact with you.

The information below will provide you with ideas for prospecting activities that you can employ to generate leads. Use the handy chart on page 233 to calculate the number of prospect contacts needed daily to achieve your goals.

Sample Prospecting Activities

Telemarketing
- For Sale By Owners / Expired Listings
- Notices of Default (Pre-foreclosure)
- Rental Community
- Past Clients
- Geographic Farm
- Banks
- Referral Sources

Face-to-Face
- Door-to-Door Neighborhood Canvasing
- Open Houses
- Networking Events
- Community Outreach
- Social Functions
- Educational Opportunities
- Booths at Events
- Past Client Pop-Bys

Marketing Tasks: Real estate marketing involves the things that you do in order to make the leads come to you. It's what you do to make the phone ring instead of you picking up the phone and making the call.

Review the list of Sample Marketing Activities on the next page and the sample marketing plan on page 235. When considering marketing tasks, include activities that you enjoy. When you prepare a marketing plan, you chart a navigable course to success.

Sample Marketing Activities

Advertising
- Newspaper/Magazines
- Radio
- Bus Stop Benches
- Shopping Carts
- Billboards
- Television
- Moving Vans

Promotional Items
- Magnets
- Calendars
- Note Pads
- Pens

Social Media
- Facebook
- Twitter
- Pinterest
- YouTube
- Google+

Direct Mail
- Postcard Campaigns
- Just Listed/Just Sold Cards
- Real Estate Market Updates
- Community Newsletters

Sponsorship
- Sports Teams
- Community Events
- Charity Events

Online Lead Generation Tools/Companies
Websites and Blogs
Voice Broadcast
Press Releases

Notes: The Notes section of the daily planner should be used to note anything that you want or need to remember. It could include phone calls, property addresses of prospects, a name of a good graphic designer—just about anything and everything that you need to run your business should be noted here. You can make additional notes on page 238.

Don't resort to writing things on sticky notes or random pieces of paper. When you keep everything in one place, you will be able to find what you need when you need it. When you use a planner, you will not need to worry about losing any random bits of information—those important items that could lead to your next successful closing.

Appointments: While many agents may use a smartphone to manage contacts and set appointments, there's always a time when you need to write notes quickly—more quickly than you can with your smartphone. Use this section to rewrite the appointments already noted in your smartphone or to jot down appointments that you set daily. If you need to do so, you can transfer all of your appointments to your smartphone later in the day.

Expenses: This is the section of every page that you should not avoid. At the end of the year, as a real estate agent, you will have many tax-deductible expenses. Have you kept good records?

While it's always a good idea to consult with your accountant with respect to your tax deductions, it's equally important to keep a record of meals with clients, mileage, office supplies, and any other costs associated with your business. When you diligently use this section of the daily planner, all you will need to do is sum up the categories and provide those totals to your accountant at tax time.

Nota bene: Don't forget to keep all of your receipts! Obtain large envelopes and label one envelope for every category of expenses. Each night, after recording your tax-deductible expenses at the bottom page, place the related receipts in the appropriate envelopes. Then, when it's time to prepare your taxes, you'll have all of the information you need in order to get the job done fast!

Highlight of the Day: Use this box to evaluate your accomplishments for the day. Remember that you are not only evaluating yourself based on the number of appointments you made or the number of listings you took. Consider how well you completed the micro-processes that will lead to more listing appointments and more sales. What moment made you feel proud? What was your finest moment?

What will you do better, stronger, faster, or differently tomorrow? There will always be someone who will be better, stronger, faster, or richer than you. Your only competition is yourself and this planner should help to challenge you to be the best YOU that you can be. It doesn't matter that the guy down the hall or at the other office takes listings like they are going out of style. Your goal is to chart a course to your personal success—which is measured by an entirely different rubric!

How to Complete the Weekly Wrap-Up Pages

Here's your opportunity to reflect on the week that just ended. Recording all that you accomplished one week will help you to get enthusiastic about the next.

Weekly Rating: This doesn't need to be a precise assessment of your daily activities. Use the 1–5 scale to record how hard you pushed yourself during the week.

Goals: Look back at the goals you set on the previous Monday. Did you meet or exceed your goals? If you frequently exceed your goals, you may need to set more challenging ones. If you are consistently falling short, consider working on micro-outcomes; make a note about why you think that you did not meet your goals.

Highlight of the Week: Look back at what you recorded as your Highlight of the Day. Select the single accomplishment that you are most proud of and record it as your Highlight of the Week. It can be anything from mastering a new technology tool to setting an appointment (or two or three).

Prospecting Notes: Assess your week as a whole, and record whether you felt that you adequately completed your prospecting tasks in order to meet your long-term goals. What went well? Which prospecting tasks did you complete most successfully?

Marketing Notes: Jot down anything significant that you accomplished in your marketing activities. How well did you complete your daily marketing tasks? Did you send out all of your direct mail? Did you reach out to your circle of influence as planned?

Networking Notes: Referrals are a large source of business for any salesperson. That's why it is vital that you network and interact with other professionals as much as possible. What activities or events did you attend this week? Did you identify any new referral sources? How can you incorporate those sources into your current business plan?

Professional Development Notes: Don't ever lose site of professional development. The real estate market is constantly changing and the tools we use in order to be successful are also continually changing. In order to stay "in the game," it's important to always develop professionally. Did you take any classes this week or attend any conferences? Were they worthwhile?

Thoughts About the Week: To achieve success in real estate in only 10 minutes a day, you must not only reflect on how well you completed your tasks, but whether you set appropriate people-oriented goals. Consider your interactions with others and how those daily interactions have helped you to chart a course to success. Note your thoughts in this section of the Weekly Wrap-Up.

The Essential Daily Planner for Real Estate Agents

Week 1

Dates: _____

Goals: _____

Monday

Prospecting Tasks

☐ _____
☐ _____
☐ _____
☐ _____
☐ _____
☐ _____

Marketing Tasks

☐ _____
☐ _____
☐ _____
☐ _____
☐ _____
☐ _____

Notes: _____

_____

_____

_____

TIME	APPOINTMENTS

HIGHLIGHT OF THE DAY

EXPENSES

Gas: _____

Meals: _____

Mileage: _____

Other: _____

_____

technology tips

Make the most of web technology, which is emerging as the key across the world and can help you promote your services to online users.

Tuesday

Prospecting Tasks

☐ _____
☐ _____
☐ _____
☐ _____
☐ _____
☐ _____

Marketing Tasks

☐ _____
☐ _____
☐ _____
☐ _____
☐ _____
☐ _____

Notes:_____
_____
_____
_____

TIME   **APPOINTMENTS**

HIGHLIGHT OF THE DAY

EXPENSES

Gas: _____
Meals: _____
Mileage: _____
Other: _____
_____

Make sure that you draw up a plan, which includes a number of qualified prospects. This will ensure less resistance when speaking about your real estate services.

Wednesday

Prospecting Tasks

- ☐ _____
- ☐ _____
- ☐ _____
- ☐ _____
- ☐ _____
- ☐ _____

Marketing Tasks

- ☐ _____
- ☐ _____
- ☐ _____
- ☐ _____
- ☐ _____
- ☐ _____

Notes: _____

_____

_____

_____

TIME   APPOINTMENTS

HIGHLIGHT OF THE DAY

EXPENSES

Gas: _____

Meals: _____

Mileage: _____

Other: _____

_____

marketing matters

Marketing materials that clearly state your value proposition make the phone ring. Print and online advertising should explain how your product will solve a problem or improve a situation.

Thursday

Prospecting Tasks

- ☐ _____
- ☐ _____
- ☐ _____
- ☐ _____
- ☐ _____
- ☐ _____

Marketing Tasks

- ☐ _____
- ☐ _____
- ☐ _____
- ☐ _____
- ☐ _____

Notes:_____
_____
_____
_____

TIME   APPOINTMENTS

HIGHLIGHT OF THE DAY

EXPENSES

Gas: _____

Meals: _____

Mileage: _____

Other: _____

_____

Online profiles on social media and networking sites are vital to the success of your personal brand. Take time to establish or update your professional profiles.

Friday

Prospecting Tasks

- ☐ _____
- ☐ _____
- ☐ _____
- ☐ _____
- ☐ _____
- ☐ _____

Marketing Tasks

- ☐ _____
- ☐ _____
- ☐ _____
- ☐ _____
- ☐ _____
- ☐ _____

Notes: _____
_____
_____
_____

TIME   APPOINTMENTS

HIGHLIGHT OF THE DAY

EXPENSES

Gas: _____

Meals: _____

Mileage: _____

Other: _____

_____

 **live and learn**

Local association marketing sessions provide an opportunity for professional development, property promotion, and networking.

Saturday

Prospecting Tasks

☐ _____
☐ _____
☐ _____
☐ _____
☐ _____
☐ _____

Marketing Tasks

☐ _____
☐ _____
☐ _____
☐ _____
☐ _____
☐ _____

Notes:_____

_____

_____

_____

TIME	APPOINTMENTS

HIGHLIGHT OF THE DAY

EXPENSES

Gas: _____

Meals: _____

Mileage: _____

Other: _____

_____

Sunday

Prospecting Tasks

☐ _____
☐ _____
☐ _____
☐ _____
☐ _____
☐ _____

Marketing Tasks

☐ _____
☐ _____
☐ _____
☐ _____
☐ _____
☐ _____

Notes: _____
_____
_____
_____

TIME   **APPOINTMENTS**

HIGHLIGHT OF THE DAY

EXPENSES

Gas: _____

Meals: _____

Mileage: _____

Other: _____

_____

Weekly Wrap-Up

GOALS:

- ☐ Met
- ☐ Exceeded
- ☐ Maybe Next Week

Highlight of the Week: _____

_____

_____

Prospecting Notes: _____

_____

_____

Marketing Notes: _____

_____

_____

Networking Notes: _____

_____

_____

Professional Development Notes: _____

_____

_____

THOUGHTS ABOUT THE WEEK

Week 2

Dates: _____

Goals: _____

Monday

Prospecting Tasks

- ☐ _____
- ☐ _____
- ☐ _____
- ☐ _____
- ☐ _____
- ☐ _____

Marketing Tasks

- ☐ _____
- ☐ _____
- ☐ _____
- ☐ _____
- ☐ _____
- ☐ _____

Notes: _____
_____
_____
_____

TIME   APPOINTMENTS

TIME	APPOINTMENTS

HIGHLIGHT OF THE DAY

EXPENSES

Gas: _____

Meals: _____

Mileage: _____

Other: _____

_____

Tuesday

Prospecting Tasks

- ☐ _____
- ☐ _____
- ☐ _____
- ☐ _____
- ☐ _____
- ☐ _____

Marketing Tasks

- ☐ _____
- ☐ _____
- ☐ _____
- ☐ _____
- ☐ _____
- ☐ _____

Notes:_____

_____

_____

_____

TIME APPOINTMENTS

HIGHLIGHT OF THE DAY

EXPENSES

Gas: _____

Meals: _____

Mileage: _____

Other: _____

_____

prospecting pointers

Cold calling is a traditional and often neglected means of generating leads. Confident callers can get the job done!

Wednesday

Prospecting Tasks

- ☐ _____
- ☐ _____
- ☐ _____
- ☐ _____
- ☐ _____
- ☐ _____

Marketing Tasks

- ☐ _____
- ☐ _____
- ☐ _____
- ☐ _____
- ☐ _____
- ☐ _____

Notes:_____

_____

_____

_____

TIME   **APPOINTMENTS**

HIGHLIGHT OF THE DAY

EXPENSES

Gas: _____

Meals: _____

Mileage: _____

Other: _____

_____

marketing matters

Organize advertising campaigns in local newspapers to market your properties. Buyers flock to local listings.

Thursday

Prospecting Tasks

- ☐ _____
- ☐ _____
- ☐ _____
- ☐ _____
- ☐ _____
- ☐ _____

Marketing Tasks

- ☐ _____
- ☐ _____
- ☐ _____
- ☐ _____
- ☐ _____
- ☐ _____

Notes: _____

_____

_____

_____

TIME   APPOINTMENTS

HIGHLIGHT OF THE DAY

EXPENSES

Gas: _____

Meals: _____

Mileage: _____

Other: _____

_____

 **success starters**

A strong database or circle of influence includes 200 contacts. Create a solid list that includes correct addresses, email information, and phone numbers.

Friday

Prospecting Tasks

- ☐ _____
- ☐ _____
- ☐ _____
- ☐ _____
- ☐ _____
- ☐ _____

Marketing Tasks

- ☐ _____
- ☐ _____
- ☐ _____
- ☐ _____
- ☐ _____
- ☐ _____

Notes: _____

_____

_____

_____

TIME   APPOINTMENTS

HIGHLIGHT OF THE DAY

EXPENSES

Gas: _____

Meals: _____

Mileage: _____

Other: _____

_____

 **live and learn**

The biggest obstacle to closing new business is managing customer objections. Listen to compact discs and review scripts to get ideas for effective objection handling.

Saturday

Prospecting Tasks

☐ _____
☐ _____
☐ _____
☐ _____
☐ _____
☐ _____

Marketing Tasks

☐ _____
☐ _____
☐ _____
☐ _____
☐ _____
☐ _____

Notes:_____
_____
_____
_____

TIME   APPOINTMENTS

HIGHLIGHT OF THE DAY

EXPENSES

Gas: _____

Meals: _____

Mileage: _____

Other: _____

_____

words of wisdom

"I've learned that people will forget what you said, people will forget what you did, but people will never forget how you made them feel."
—Maya Angelou, American author and poet

Sunday

Prospecting Tasks

☐ _____
☐ _____
☐ _____
☐ _____
☐ _____
☐ _____

Marketing Tasks

☐ _____
☐ _____
☐ _____
☐ _____
☐ _____
☐ _____

Notes: _____
_____
_____
_____

TIME   **APPOINTMENTS**

HIGHLIGHT OF THE DAY

EXPENSES

Gas: _____

Meals: _____

Mileage: _____

Other: _____

_____

Weekly Wrap-Up

WEEKLY RATING

GOALS:

☐ Met

☐ Exceeded

☐ Maybe Next Week

Highlight of the Week: _____

_____

_____

Prospecting Notes: _____

_____

_____

Marketing Notes: _____

_____

_____

Networking Notes: _____

_____

_____

Professional Development Notes: _____

_____

_____

THOUGHTS ABOUT THE WEEK

Week 3

Dates: _____

Goals: _____

Monday

Prospecting Tasks

☐ _____
☐ _____
☐ _____
☐ _____
☐ _____
☐ _____

Marketing Tasks

☐ _____
☐ _____
☐ _____
☐ _____
☐ _____
☐ _____

Notes:_____
_____
_____
_____

TIME   APPOINTMENTS

HIGHLIGHT OF THE DAY

EXPENSES

Gas: _____

Meals: _____

Mileage: _____

Other: _____

_____

technology tips

Nowadays, media and its advances are making a gigantic leap, so it's a good idea to use this technology to promote your local listings.

Tuesday

Prospecting Tasks

- ☐ _____
- ☐ _____
- ☐ _____
- ☐ _____
- ☐ _____
- ☐ _____

Marketing Tasks

- ☐ _____
- ☐ _____
- ☐ _____
- ☐ _____
- ☐ _____
- ☐ _____

Notes:_____

_____

_____

_____

TIME   APPOINTMENTS

HIGHLIGHT OF THE DAY

EXPENSES

Gas: _____

Meals: _____

Mileage: _____

Other: _____

_____

Wednesday

Prospecting Tasks

- ☐ _____
- ☐ _____
- ☐ _____
- ☐ _____
- ☐ _____
- ☐ _____

Marketing Tasks

- ☐ _____
- ☐ _____
- ☐ _____
- ☐ _____
- ☐ _____
- ☐ _____

Notes:_____

_____

_____

_____

TIME	APPOINTMENTS

HIGHLIGHT OF THE DAY

EXPENSES

Gas: _____

Meals: _____

Mileage: _____

Other: _____

_____

marketing matters

Remember to always advertise the benefits of your services. Outline the differences between your services and those of your competition.

Thursday

Prospecting Tasks

- ☐ _____
- ☐ _____
- ☐ _____
- ☐ _____
- ☐ _____
- ☐ _____

Marketing Tasks

- ☐ _____
- ☐ _____
- ☐ _____
- ☐ _____
- ☐ _____
- ☐ _____

Notes:_____

_____

_____

_____

TIME   **APPOINTMENTS**

HIGHLIGHT OF THE DAY

EXPENSES

Gas: _____

Meals: _____

Mileage: _____

Other: _____

_____

success starters

Review, update, or complete the contact information that is stored in your smartphone or customer relationship management program.

Friday

Prospecting Tasks

- ☐ _____
- ☐ _____
- ☐ _____
- ☐ _____
- ☐ _____
- ☐ _____

Marketing Tasks

- ☐ _____
- ☐ _____
- ☐ _____
- ☐ _____
- ☐ _____
- ☐ _____

Notes:_____

_____

_____

_____

TIME	APPOINTMENTS

HIGHLIGHT OF THE DAY

EXPENSES

Gas: _____

Meals: _____

Mileage: _____

Other: _____

_____

Saturday

Prospecting Tasks

- ☐ _____
- ☐ _____
- ☐ _____
- ☐ _____
- ☐ _____
- ☐ _____

Marketing Tasks

- ☐ _____
- ☐ _____
- ☐ _____
- ☐ _____
- ☐ _____
- ☐ _____

Notes:_____

_____

_____

_____

TIME   APPOINTMENTS

HIGHLIGHT OF THE DAY

EXPENSES

Gas: _____

Meals: _____

Mileage: _____

Other: _____

_____

 **words of wisdom** "The competitor to be feared is one who never bothers about you at all, but goes on making his own business better all the time." —Henry Ford, founder of Ford Motor Company

Sunday

Prospecting Tasks

- [ ] _____
- [ ] _____
- [ ] _____
- [ ] _____
- [ ] _____
- [ ] _____

Marketing Tasks

- [ ] _____
- [ ] _____
- [ ] _____
- [ ] _____
- [ ] _____
- [ ] _____

Notes:_____
_____
_____
_____

TIME   APPOINTMENTS

HIGHLIGHT OF THE DAY

EXPENSES

Gas: _____

Meals: _____

Mileage: _____

Other: _____

_____

Weekly Wrap-Up

GOALS:

- ☐ Met
- ☐ Exceeded
- ☐ Maybe Next Week

Highlight of the Week: _____
_____
_____

Prospecting Notes: _____
_____
_____

Marketing Notes: _____
_____
_____

Networking Notes: _____
_____
_____

Professional Development Notes: _____
_____
_____

THOUGHTS ABOUT THE WEEK

Week 4

Dates: _____

Goals: _____

Monday

Prospecting Tasks

- ☐ _____
- ☐ _____
- ☐ _____
- ☐ _____
- ☐ _____
- ☐ _____

Marketing Tasks

- ☐ _____
- ☐ _____
- ☐ _____
- ☐ _____
- ☐ _____
- ☐ _____

Notes: _____
_____
_____
_____

TIME	APPOINTMENTS

HIGHLIGHT OF THE DAY

EXPENSES

Gas: _____

Meals: _____

Mileage: _____

Other: _____

_____

technology tips

Emails serve as a quick and professional way to communicate with hundreds of users. A campaign through email is considered to be very efficient and cost-effective.

Tuesday

Prospecting Tasks

- ☐ _____
- ☐ _____
- ☐ _____
- ☐ _____
- ☐ _____
- ☐ _____

Marketing Tasks

- ☐ _____
- ☐ _____
- ☐ _____
- ☐ _____
- ☐ _____
- ☐ _____

Notes:_____

_____

_____

_____

TIME   APPOINTMENTS

HIGHLIGHT OF THE DAY

EXPENSES

Gas: _____

Meals: _____

Mileage: _____

Other: _____

_____

prospecting pointers

Try instilling the right attitude among your sales team. This can help to motivate them and result in favorable relationships with customers.

Wednesday

Prospecting Tasks

- ☐ _____
- ☐ _____
- ☐ _____
- ☐ _____
- ☐ _____
- ☐ _____

Marketing Tasks

- ☐ _____
- ☐ _____
- ☐ _____
- ☐ _____
- ☐ _____
- ☐ _____

Notes: _____

_____

_____

_____

TIME   APPOINTMENTS

HIGHLIGHT OF THE DAY

EXPENSES

Gas: _____

Meals: _____

Mileage: _____

Other: _____

_____

 **marketing matters**

Hire a graphic designer to create pamphlets, flyers, and brochures that effectively and attractively market your property listings and your real estate services.

Thursday

Prospecting Tasks

- ☐ _____
- ☐ _____
- ☐ _____
- ☐ _____
- ☐ _____
- ☐ _____

Marketing Tasks

- ☐ _____
- ☐ _____
- ☐ _____
- ☐ _____
- ☐ _____
- ☐ _____

Notes:_____
_____
_____
_____

TIME   APPOINTMENTS

HIGHLIGHT OF THE DAY

EXPENSES

Gas: _____

Meals: _____

Mileage: _____

Other: _____

_____

Friday

Prospecting Tasks

- ☐ _____
- ☐ _____
- ☐ _____
- ☐ _____
- ☐ _____
- ☐ _____

Marketing Tasks

- ☐ _____
- ☐ _____
- ☐ _____
- ☐ _____
- ☐ _____
- ☐ _____

Notes:_____

_____

_____

_____

TIME   APPOINTMENTS

HIGHLIGHT OF THE DAY

EXPENSES

Gas: _____

Meals: _____

Mileage: _____

Other: _____

_____

 **live and learn**

Ask each person you meet for two cards—one to pass on to someone else and one to keep. This sets the stage for networking to happen.

Saturday

Prospecting Tasks

- ☐ _____
- ☐ _____
- ☐ _____
- ☐ _____
- ☐ _____
- ☐ _____

Marketing Tasks

- ☐ _____
- ☐ _____
- ☐ _____
- ☐ _____
- ☐ _____
- ☐ _____

Notes:_____

_____

_____

_____

TIME	APPOINTMENTS

HIGHLIGHT OF THE DAY

EXPENSES

Gas: _____

Meals: _____

Mileage: _____

Other: _____

_____

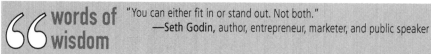
Sunday

Prospecting Tasks

- ☐ _____
- ☐ _____
- ☐ _____
- ☐ _____
- ☐ _____
- ☐ _____

Marketing Tasks

- ☐ _____
- ☐ _____
- ☐ _____
- ☐ _____
- ☐ _____
- ☐ _____

Notes:_____

_____

_____

_____

TIME	APPOINTMENTS

HIGHLIGHT OF THE DAY

EXPENSES

Gas: _____

Meals: _____

Mileage: _____

Other: _____

_____

Weekly Wrap-Up

GOALS:

☐ Met

☐ Exceeded

☐ Maybe Next Week

Highlight of the Week: _____
_____
_____

Prospecting Notes: _____
_____
_____

Marketing Notes: _____
_____
_____

Networking Notes: _____
_____
_____

Professional Development Notes: _____
_____
_____

THOUGHTS ABOUT THE WEEK

Week 5

Dates: _____

Goals: _____

Monday

Prospecting Tasks

- ☐ _____
- ☐ _____
- ☐ _____
- ☐ _____
- ☐ _____
- ☐ _____

Marketing Tasks

- ☐ _____
- ☐ _____
- ☐ _____
- ☐ _____
- ☐ _____
- ☐ _____

Notes: _____

_____

_____

_____

TIME	APPOINTMENTS

HIGHLIGHT OF THE DAY

EXPENSES

Gas: _____

Meals: _____

Mileage: _____

Other: _____

_____

technology tips

"A picture is worth a thousand words." Statistics show that photos and videos have a stronger online presence than text. Upload videos and photos to advertise through digital media.

Tuesday

Prospecting Tasks

- ☐ _____
- ☐ _____
- ☐ _____
- ☐ _____
- ☐ _____
- ☐ _____

Marketing Tasks

- ☐ _____
- ☐ _____
- ☐ _____
- ☐ _____
- ☐ _____
- ☐ _____

Notes:_____
_____
_____
_____

TIME   **APPOINTMENTS**

HIGHLIGHT OF THE DAY

EXPENSES

Gas: _____

Meals: _____

Mileage: _____

Other: _____

_____

prospecting pointers

Empower associates, employees, and referral partners, so that they can share the benefits of your real estate service with potential customers.

Wednesday

Prospecting Tasks

- ☐ _____
- ☐ _____
- ☐ _____
- ☐ _____
- ☐ _____
- ☐ _____

Marketing Tasks

- ☐ _____
- ☐ _____
- ☐ _____
- ☐ _____
- ☐ _____
- ☐ _____

Notes:_____

_____

_____

_____

TIME   APPOINTMENTS

HIGHLIGHT OF THE DAY

EXPENSES

Gas: _____

Meals: _____

Mileage: _____

Other: _____

_____

marketing matters

The U.S. Postal Service® offers affordable direct mail marketing that includes online demographic filters for target market management. You don't even need a recipient's mailing address to use this service.

Thursday

Prospecting Tasks

- [ ] _____
- [ ] _____
- [ ] _____
- [ ] _____
- [ ] _____
- [ ] _____

Marketing Tasks

- [ ] _____
- [ ] _____
- [ ] _____
- [ ] _____
- [ ] _____
- [ ] _____

Notes:_____

_____

_____

_____

TIME   APPOINTMENTS

HIGHLIGHT OF THE DAY

EXPENSES

Gas:_____

Meals:_____

Mileage:_____

Other:_____

_____

Using the MLS hot sheets will make you aware of the latest market changes in your area. Set up your MLS preferences, and check your hot sheets daily.

Friday

Prospecting Tasks

☐ _____
☐ _____
☐ _____
☐ _____
☐ _____
☐ _____

Marketing Tasks

☐ _____
☐ _____
☐ _____
☐ _____
☐ _____
☐ _____

Notes: _____

_____

_____

_____

TIME   APPOINTMENTS

HIGHLIGHT OF THE DAY

EXPENSES

Gas: _____

Meals: _____

Mileage: _____

Other: _____

_____

**live and learn**

Active partnerships with other local businesses can open the doors to increased opportunities and new clients.

Saturday

Prospecting Tasks

- ☐ _____
- ☐ _____
- ☐ _____
- ☐ _____
- ☐ _____
- ☐ _____

Marketing Tasks

- ☐ _____
- ☐ _____
- ☐ _____
- ☐ _____
- ☐ _____
- ☐ _____

Notes:_____

_____

_____

_____

TIME   APPOINTMENTS

HIGHLIGHT OF THE DAY

EXPENSES

Gas: _____

Meals: _____

Mileage: _____

Other: _____

_____

words of wisdom

"Don't compromise yourself. You're all you've got."
—Janis Joplin, singer-songwriter who rose to fame in the late 1960s

Sunday

Prospecting Tasks

☐ _____
☐ _____
☐ _____
☐ _____
☐ _____
☐ _____

Marketing Tasks

☐ _____
☐ _____
☐ _____
☐ _____
☐ _____
☐ _____

Notes: _____
_____
_____
_____

TIME   APPOINTMENTS

HIGHLIGHT OF THE DAY

EXPENSES

Gas: _____

Meals: _____

Mileage: _____

Other: _____

_____

Weekly Wrap-Up

GOALS:

- ☐ Met
- ☐ Exceeded
- ☐ Maybe Next Week

Highlight of the Week: _____
_____
_____

Prospecting Notes: _____
_____
_____

Marketing Notes: _____
_____
_____

Networking Notes: _____
_____
_____

Professional Development Notes: _____
_____
_____

THOUGHTS ABOUT THE WEEK

Week 6

Dates: _____

Goals: _____

Monday

Prospecting Tasks

- ☐ _____
- ☐ _____
- ☐ _____
- ☐ _____
- ☐ _____
- ☐ _____

Marketing Tasks

- ☐ _____
- ☐ _____
- ☐ _____
- ☐ _____
- ☐ _____
- ☐ _____

Notes: _____

_____

_____

_____

TIME	APPOINTMENTS

HIGHLIGHT OF THE DAY

EXPENSES

Gas: _____

Meals: _____

Mileage: _____

Other: _____

_____

technology tips

A well-crafted online advertising campaign can gain increased exposure for your brand and your services.

Tuesday

Prospecting Tasks

- ☐ _____
- ☐ _____
- ☐ _____
- ☐ _____
- ☐ _____
- ☐ _____

Marketing Tasks

- ☐ _____
- ☐ _____
- ☐ _____
- ☐ _____
- ☐ _____
- ☐ _____

Notes: _____

_____

_____

_____

TIME   **APPOINTMENTS**

HIGHLIGHT OF THE DAY

EXPENSES

Gas: _____

Meals: _____

Mileage: _____

Other: _____

_____

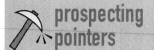

prospecting pointers

Invest in acquiring databases with the contact details of your target audience. Good lists are current and up-to-date. Using a well-constructed database can lead to increased lead conversion.

Wednesday

Prospecting Tasks

- ☐ _____
- ☐ _____
- ☐ _____
- ☐ _____
- ☐ _____
- ☐ _____

Marketing Tasks

- ☐ _____
- ☐ _____
- ☐ _____
- ☐ _____
- ☐ _____
- ☐ _____

Notes:_____

_____

_____

_____

TIME **APPOINTMENTS**

HIGHLIGHT OF THE DAY

EXPENSES

Gas: _____

Meals: _____

Mileage: _____

Other: _____

_____

Create promotional products to generate top of mind awareness. T-shirts, phone chargers, and even mobile phone cleaning products are popular items that increase brand recognition.

Thursday

Prospecting Tasks

- [ ] _____
- [ ] _____
- [ ] _____
- [ ] _____
- [ ] _____
- [ ] _____

Marketing Tasks

- [ ] _____
- [ ] _____
- [ ] _____
- [ ] _____
- [ ] _____
- [ ] _____

Notes:_____

_____

_____

_____

TIME   **APPOINTMENTS**

HIGHLIGHT OF THE DAY

EXPENSES

Gas: _____

Meals: _____

Mileage: _____

Other: _____

_____

success starters

Use the Multiple Listing Service to select five homes for sale in your market area. Preview these homes to increase your market knowledge.

Friday

Prospecting Tasks

- ☐ _____
- ☐ _____
- ☐ _____
- ☐ _____
- ☐ _____
- ☐ _____

Marketing Tasks

- ☐ _____
- ☐ _____
- ☐ _____
- ☐ _____
- ☐ _____
- ☐ _____

Notes: _____

_____

_____

_____

TIME	APPOINTMENTS

HIGHLIGHT OF THE DAY

EXPENSES

Gas: _____

Meals: _____

Mileage: _____

Other: _____

_____

 **live and learn**

Saturday

Prospecting Tasks

☐ _____
☐ _____
☐ _____
☐ _____
☐ _____
☐ _____

Marketing Tasks

☐ _____
☐ _____
☐ _____
☐ _____
☐ _____
☐ _____

Notes:_____
_____
_____
_____

TIME   APPOINTMENTS

HIGHLIGHT OF THE DAY

EXPENSES

Gas: _____
Meals: _____
Mileage: _____
Other: _____
_____

Sunday

Prospecting Tasks

☐ _____
☐ _____
☐ _____
☐ _____
☐ _____
☐ _____

Marketing Tasks

☐ _____
☐ _____
☐ _____
☐ _____
☐ _____
☐ _____

Notes: _____
_____
_____
_____

TIME   APPOINTMENTS

HIGHLIGHT OF THE DAY

EXPENSES

Gas: _____

Meals: _____

Mileage: _____

Other: _____

_____

Weekly Wrap-Up

GOALS:

☐ Met

☐ Exceeded

☐ Maybe Next Week

Highlight of the Week: _____

_____

_____

Prospecting Notes: _____

_____

_____

Marketing Notes: _____

_____

_____

Networking Notes: _____

_____

_____

Professional Development Notes: _____

_____

_____

THOUGHTS ABOUT THE WEEK

Week 7

Dates: _____

Goals: _____

Monday

Prospecting Tasks

- ☐ _____
- ☐ _____
- ☐ _____
- ☐ _____
- ☐ _____
- ☐ _____

Marketing Tasks

- ☐ _____
- ☐ _____
- ☐ _____
- ☐ _____
- ☐ _____
- ☐ _____

Notes: _____

_____

_____

_____

TIME	APPOINTMENTS

HIGHLIGHT OF THE DAY

EXPENSES

Gas: _____

Meals: _____

Mileage: _____

Other: _____

_____

Tuesday

Prospecting Tasks

- ☐ _____
- ☐ _____
- ☐ _____
- ☐ _____
- ☐ _____
- ☐ _____

Marketing Tasks

- ☐ _____
- ☐ _____
- ☐ _____
- ☐ _____
- ☐ _____
- ☐ _____

Notes: _____

_____

_____

_____

TIME   APPOINTMENTS

HIGHLIGHT OF THE DAY

EXPENSES

Gas: _____

Meals: _____

Mileage: _____

Other: _____

_____

 **prospecting pointers**

Often we neglect what we have; hence this is the time for you to dig through your business book and telephone some of your past clients.

Wednesday

Prospecting Tasks

- ☐ _____
- ☐ _____
- ☐ _____
- ☐ _____
- ☐ _____
- ☐ _____

Marketing Tasks

- ☐ _____
- ☐ _____
- ☐ _____
- ☐ _____
- ☐ _____
- ☐ _____

Notes:_____

_____

_____

_____

TIME   APPOINTMENTS

HIGHLIGHT OF THE DAY

EXPENSES

Gas: _____

Meals: _____

Mileage: _____

Other: _____

_____

marketing matters

Referral or word-of-mouth marketing can be extremely effective. When you build goodwill and create trust, your circle of influence will spread the word.

Thursday

Prospecting Tasks

- [ ] _____
- [ ] _____
- [ ] _____
- [ ] _____
- [ ] _____
- [ ] _____

Marketing Tasks

- [ ] _____
- [ ] _____
- [ ] _____
- [ ] _____
- [ ] _____
- [ ] _____

Notes:_____

_____

_____

_____

TIME	APPOINTMENTS

HIGHLIGHT OF THE DAY

EXPENSES

Gas: _____

Meals: _____

Mileage: _____

Other: _____

_____

Obtain permission from your broker or other agents in the office to market their listings online. Create online classified ads on sites such as Craigslist in order to generate new buyers.

Friday

Prospecting Tasks

☐ _____
☐ _____
☐ _____
☐ _____
☐ _____
☐ _____

Marketing Tasks

☐ _____
☐ _____
☐ _____
☐ _____
☐ _____
☐ _____

Notes: _____
_____
_____
_____

TIME   APPOINTMENTS

HIGHLIGHT OF THE DAY

EXPENSES

Gas: _____

Meals: _____

Mileage: _____

Other: _____

_____

 **live and learn**

Social media sites such as Facebook and LinkedIn make it easy to foster new relationships and identify new referral partners.

Saturday

Prospecting Tasks

☐ _____
☐ _____
☐ _____
☐ _____
☐ _____
☐ _____

Marketing Tasks

☐ _____
☐ _____
☐ _____
☐ _____
☐ _____
☐ _____

Notes:_____
_____
_____
_____

TIME   APPOINTMENTS

HIGHLIGHT OF THE DAY

EXPENSES

Gas: _____
Meals: _____
Mileage: _____
Other: _____
_____

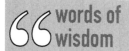

Sunday

Prospecting Tasks

☐ _____
☐ _____
☐ _____
☐ _____
☐ _____
☐ _____

Marketing Tasks

☐ _____
☐ _____
☐ _____
☐ _____
☐ _____
☐ _____

Notes: _____

_____

_____

_____

TIME	APPOINTMENTS

HIGHLIGHT OF THE DAY

EXPENSES

Gas: _____

Meals: _____

Mileage: _____

Other: _____

_____

Weekly Wrap-Up

GOALS:

☐ Met

☐ Exceeded

☐ Maybe Next Week

Highlight of the Week: _____

_____

_____

Prospecting Notes: _____

_____

_____

Marketing Notes: _____

_____

_____

Networking Notes: _____

_____

_____

Professional Development Notes: _____

_____

_____

THOUGHTS ABOUT THE WEEK

Week 8

Dates: _____

Goals: _____

Monday

Prospecting Tasks

☐ _____
☐ _____
☐ _____
☐ _____
☐ _____
☐ _____

Marketing Tasks

☐ _____
☐ _____
☐ _____
☐ _____
☐ _____
☐ _____

Notes: _____
_____
_____
_____

TIME	APPOINTMENTS

HIGHLIGHT OF THE DAY

EXPENSES

Gas: _____

Meals: _____

Mileage: _____

Other: _____

_____

technology tips

Pop-ups over Internet websites have proven to be effective in attracting the attention of online users; your business can take advantage of this technological offshoot.

Tuesday

Prospecting Tasks

- ☐ _____
- ☐ _____
- ☐ _____
- ☐ _____
- ☐ _____
- ☐ _____

Marketing Tasks

- ☐ _____
- ☐ _____
- ☐ _____
- ☐ _____
- ☐ _____
- ☐ _____

Notes:_____

_____

_____

_____

TIME   **APPOINTMENTS**

HIGHLIGHT OF THE DAY

EXPENSES

Gas: _____

Meals: _____

Mileage: _____

Other: _____

_____

prospecting pointers Call prospects several times a year to present them with attractive offers.

Wednesday

Prospecting Tasks

- ☐ _____
- ☐ _____
- ☐ _____
- ☐ _____
- ☐ _____
- ☐ _____

Marketing Tasks

- ☐ _____
- ☐ _____
- ☐ _____
- ☐ _____
- ☐ _____
- ☐ _____

Notes:_____

_____

_____

_____

TIME	APPOINTMENTS

HIGHLIGHT OF THE DAY

EXPENSES

Gas: _____

Meals: _____

Mileage: _____

Other: _____

_____

Can you ask for a more effective means of marketing than online these days? Unleash the power of the web to locate new buyers and sellers that need your services today.

Thursday

Prospecting Tasks

- ☐ _____
- ☐ _____
- ☐ _____
- ☐ _____
- ☐ _____
- ☐ _____

Marketing Tasks

- ☐ _____
- ☐ _____
- ☐ _____
- ☐ _____
- ☐ _____
- ☐ _____

Notes:_____

_____

_____

_____

TIME   APPOINTMENTS

HIGHLIGHT OF THE DAY

EXPENSES

Gas: _____

Meals: _____

Mileage: _____

Other: _____

_____

success starters

If you do not already have one, select a farm area. Learn about the architectural styles and streets in the neighborhood, and preview homes currently for sale.

Friday

Prospecting Tasks

☐ _____
☐ _____
☐ _____
☐ _____
☐ _____
☐ _____

Marketing Tasks

☐ _____
☐ _____
☐ _____
☐ _____
☐ _____
☐ _____

Notes: _____
_____
_____
_____

TIME   APPOINTMENTS

HIGHLIGHT OF THE DAY

EXPENSES

Gas: _____

Meals: _____

Mileage: _____

Other: _____

_____

 **live and learn**

Host an annual or seasonal party for past clients, affiliates, and your referral network; this will help to maintain top of mind awareness and generate future business.

Saturday

Prospecting Tasks

- ☐ _____
- ☐ _____
- ☐ _____
- ☐ _____
- ☐ _____
- ☐ _____

Marketing Tasks

- ☐ _____
- ☐ _____
- ☐ _____
- ☐ _____
- ☐ _____
- ☐ _____

Notes:_____

_____

_____

_____

TIME   APPOINTMENTS

HIGHLIGHT OF THE DAY

EXPENSES

Gas: _____

Meals: _____

Mileage: _____

Other: _____

_____

Sunday

Prospecting Tasks

- ☐ _____
- ☐ _____
- ☐ _____
- ☐ _____
- ☐ _____
- ☐ _____

Marketing Tasks

- ☐ _____
- ☐ _____
- ☐ _____
- ☐ _____
- ☐ _____
- ☐ _____

Notes: _____

_____

_____

_____

TIME   **APPOINTMENTS**

HIGHLIGHT OF THE DAY

EXPENSES

Gas: _____

Meals: _____

Mileage: _____

Other: _____

_____

Weekly Wrap-Up

GOALS:

- ☐ Met
- ☐ Exceeded
- ☐ Maybe Next Week

Highlight of the Week: _____
_____
_____

Prospecting Notes: _____
_____
_____

Marketing Notes: _____
_____
_____

Networking Notes: _____
_____
_____

Professional Development Notes: _____
_____
_____

THOUGHTS ABOUT THE WEEK

Week 9

Dates: _____

Goals: _____

Monday

Prospecting Tasks

- ☐ _____
- ☐ _____
- ☐ _____
- ☐ _____
- ☐ _____
- ☐ _____

Marketing Tasks

- ☐ _____
- ☐ _____
- ☐ _____
- ☐ _____
- ☐ _____
- ☐ _____

Notes:_____
_____
_____
_____

TIME	APPOINTMENTS

HIGHLIGHT OF THE DAY

EXPENSES

Gas: _____

Meals: _____

Mileage: _____

Other: _____

_____

technology tips

Increasingly, Internet users are turning towards websites where consumers review products and services. Work to establish positive online reviews.

Tuesday

Prospecting Tasks

- ☐ _____
- ☐ _____
- ☐ _____
- ☐ _____
- ☐ _____
- ☐ _____

Marketing Tasks

- ☐ _____
- ☐ _____
- ☐ _____
- ☐ _____
- ☐ _____
- ☐ _____

Notes:_____

_____

_____

_____

TIME   **APPOINTMENTS**

HIGHLIGHT OF THE DAY

EXPENSES

Gas: _____

Meals: _____

Mileage: _____

Other: _____

_____

Wednesday

Prospecting Tasks

- ☐ _____
- ☐ _____
- ☐ _____
- ☐ _____
- ☐ _____
- ☐ _____

Marketing Tasks

- ☐ _____
- ☐ _____
- ☐ _____
- ☐ _____
- ☐ _____
- ☐ _____

Notes:_____
_____
_____
_____

TIME   APPOINTMENTS

HIGHLIGHT OF THE DAY

EXPENSES

Gas: _____

Meals: _____

Mileage: _____

Other: _____

_____

 marketing matters

A well-written and well-presented radio ad that discusses the benefits of your services can generate hundreds of leads.

Thursday

Prospecting Tasks

- ☐ _____
- ☐ _____
- ☐ _____
- ☐ _____
- ☐ _____
- ☐ _____

Marketing Tasks

- ☐ _____
- ☐ _____
- ☐ _____
- ☐ _____
- ☐ _____
- ☐ _____

Notes: _____

_____

_____

_____

TIME   APPOINTMENTS

HIGHLIGHT OF THE DAY

EXPENSES

Gas: _____

Meals: _____

Mileage: _____

Other: _____

_____

success starters

There are many online platforms that allow you to submit a free press release. Write a press release that announces any of your new services, awards, or achievements.

Friday

Prospecting Tasks

☐ _____
☐ _____
☐ _____
☐ _____
☐ _____
☐ _____

Marketing Tasks

☐ _____
☐ _____
☐ _____
☐ _____
☐ _____
☐ _____

Notes:_____
_____
_____
_____

TIME   APPOINTMENTS

HIGHLIGHT OF THE DAY

EXPENSES

Gas: _____

Meals: _____

Mileage: _____

Other: _____

_____

 **live and learn**

Your local Realtor® association offers many workshops and educational opportunities. Take advantage and head to the top of the class.

Saturday

Prospecting Tasks

- [ ] _____
- [ ] _____
- [ ] _____
- [ ] _____
- [ ] _____
- [ ] _____

Marketing Tasks

- [ ] _____
- [ ] _____
- [ ] _____
- [ ] _____
- [ ] _____
- [ ] _____

Notes:_____

_____

_____

_____

TIME   APPOINTMENTS

HIGHLIGHT OF THE DAY

EXPENSES

Gas: _____

Meals: _____

Mileage: _____

Other: _____

_____

words of wisdom

"In the middle of every difficulty lies opportunity."
—Albert Einstein, German physicist who developed
the theory of relativity

Sunday

Prospecting Tasks

- ☐ _____
- ☐ _____
- ☐ _____
- ☐ _____
- ☐ _____
- ☐ _____

Marketing Tasks

- ☐ _____
- ☐ _____
- ☐ _____
- ☐ _____
- ☐ _____
- ☐ _____

Notes:_____
_____
_____
_____

TIME   **APPOINTMENTS**

HIGHLIGHT OF THE DAY

EXPENSES

Gas: _____

Meals: _____

Mileage: _____

Other: _____

_____

Weekly Wrap-Up

GOALS:

- ☐ Met
- ☐ Exceeded
- ☐ Maybe Next Week

Highlight of the Week: _____
_____
_____

Prospecting Notes: _____
_____
_____

Marketing Notes: _____
_____
_____

Networking Notes: _____
_____
_____

Professional Development Notes: _____
_____
_____

THOUGHTS ABOUT THE WEEK

Week 10

Dates: _____

Goals: _____

Monday

Prospecting Tasks

- [ ] _____
- [ ] _____
- [ ] _____
- [ ] _____
- [ ] _____
- [ ] _____

Marketing Tasks

- [ ] _____
- [ ] _____
- [ ] _____
- [ ] _____
- [ ] _____
- [ ] _____

Notes:_____

_____

_____

_____

TIME	APPOINTMENTS

HIGHLIGHT OF THE DAY

EXPENSES

Gas: _____

Meals: _____

Mileage: _____

Other: _____

_____

technology tips

Digital printing has grown by leaps and bounds; it's easy and affordable to get your flyers and brochures printed and delivered through an online provider.

Tuesday

Prospecting Tasks

- ☐ _____
- ☐ _____
- ☐ _____
- ☐ _____
- ☐ _____
- ☐ _____

Marketing Tasks

- ☐ _____
- ☐ _____
- ☐ _____
- ☐ _____
- ☐ _____
- ☐ _____

Notes:_____
_____
_____
_____

TIME   APPOINTMENTS

HIGHLIGHT OF THE DAY

EXPENSES

Gas: _____

Meals: _____

Mileage: _____

Other: _____

_____

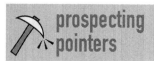

prospecting pointers

It is possible that most people you call may not acquiesce the first time. However, you must persist with confidence in your business.

Wednesday

Prospecting Tasks

- ☐ _____
- ☐ _____
- ☐ _____
- ☐ _____
- ☐ _____
- ☐ _____

Marketing Tasks

- ☐ _____
- ☐ _____
- ☐ _____
- ☐ _____
- ☐ _____
- ☐ _____

Notes:_____

_____

_____

_____

TIME   APPOINTMENTS

HIGHLIGHT OF THE DAY

EXPENSES

Gas: _____

Meals: _____

Mileage: _____

Other: _____

_____

 **marketing matters**

Billboard advertising along roads and highways can capture the attention of travelers and commuters. An attractive and clever campaign can generate the right results.

Thursday

Prospecting Tasks

- ☐ _____
- ☐ _____
- ☐ _____
- ☐ _____
- ☐ _____
- ☐ _____

Marketing Tasks

- ☐ _____
- ☐ _____
- ☐ _____
- ☐ _____
- ☐ _____
- ☐ _____

Notes:_____

_____

_____

_____

TIME | **APPOINTMENTS**

HIGHLIGHT OF THE DAY

EXPENSES

Gas: _____

Meals: _____

Mileage: _____

Other: _____

_____

success starters

Working with a new software program or platform? Watch training videos on YouTube to assist in achieving mastery.

Friday

Prospecting Tasks

- [ ] _____
- [ ] _____
- [ ] _____
- [ ] _____
- [ ] _____
- [ ] _____

Marketing Tasks

- [ ] _____
- [ ] _____
- [ ] _____
- [ ] _____
- [ ] _____
- [ ] _____

Notes:_____

_____

_____

_____

TIME   APPOINTMENTS

HIGHLIGHT OF THE DAY

EXPENSES

Gas: _____

Meals: _____

Mileage: _____

Other: _____

_____

 **live and learn**

Your brokerage has a financial interest in your success. Communicate your professional development needs with your office manager, who can organize classes for you and the other agents.

Saturday

Prospecting Tasks

- ☐ _____
- ☐ _____
- ☐ _____
- ☐ _____
- ☐ _____
- ☐ _____

Marketing Tasks

- ☐ _____
- ☐ _____
- ☐ _____
- ☐ _____
- ☐ _____
- ☐ _____

Notes:_____
_____
_____
_____

TIME   APPOINTMENTS

HIGHLIGHT OF THE DAY

EXPENSES

Gas: _____

Meals: _____

Mileage: _____

Other: _____

_____

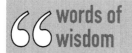

words of wisdom

"It is never too late to be what you might have been."
—George Eliot, English novelist, journalist, and translator during the Victorian era

Sunday

Prospecting Tasks

☐ _____
☐ _____
☐ _____
☐ _____
☐ _____
☐ _____

Marketing Tasks

☐ _____
☐ _____
☐ _____
☐ _____
☐ _____
☐ _____

Notes: _____
_____
_____
_____

TIME   **APPOINTMENTS**

HIGHLIGHT OF THE DAY

EXPENSES

Gas: _____

Meals: _____

Mileage: _____

Other: _____

_____

Weekly Wrap-Up

GOALS:

☐ Met

☐ Exceeded

☐ Maybe Next Week

Highlight of the Week: _____
_____
_____

Prospecting Notes: _____
_____
_____

Marketing Notes: _____
_____
_____

Networking Notes: _____
_____
_____

Professional Development Notes: _____
_____
_____

THOUGHTS ABOUT THE WEEK

Week 11

Dates: _____

Goals: _____

Monday

Prospecting Tasks

- ☐ _____
- ☐ _____
- ☐ _____
- ☐ _____
- ☐ _____
- ☐ _____

Marketing Tasks

- ☐ _____
- ☐ _____
- ☐ _____
- ☐ _____
- ☐ _____
- ☐ _____

Notes: _____
_____
_____
_____

TIME	APPOINTMENTS

HIGHLIGHT OF THE DAY

EXPENSES

Gas: _____

Meals: _____

Mileage: _____

Other: _____

_____

technology tips

In contrast with previous generation screens, LED technology causes viewers to focus more on what is displayed. Consider how your real estate marketing can reap benefits of LED advertising.

Tuesday

Prospecting Tasks

- ☐ _____
- ☐ _____
- ☐ _____
- ☐ _____
- ☐ _____
- ☐ _____

Marketing Tasks

- ☐ _____
- ☐ _____
- ☐ _____
- ☐ _____
- ☐ _____
- ☐ _____

Notes: _____

_____

_____

_____

TIME   APPOINTMENTS

HIGHLIGHT OF THE DAY

EXPENSES

Gas: _____

Meals: _____

Mileage: _____

Other: _____

_____

Wednesday

Prospecting Tasks

- ☐ _____
- ☐ _____
- ☐ _____
- ☐ _____
- ☐ _____
- ☐ _____

Marketing Tasks

- ☐ _____
- ☐ _____
- ☐ _____
- ☐ _____
- ☐ _____
- ☐ _____

Notes:_____

_____

_____

_____

TIME	APPOINTMENTS

HIGHLIGHT OF THE DAY

EXPENSES

Gas: _____

Meals: _____

Mileage: _____

Other: _____

_____

marketing matters

Google Adsense and other online pay-per-click advertising can increase the visibility of your real estate business. Benefits include maximum local exposure and a small initial investment.

Thursday

Prospecting Tasks

- ☐ _____
- ☐ _____
- ☐ _____
- ☐ _____
- ☐ _____
- ☐ _____

Marketing Tasks

- ☐ _____
- ☐ _____
- ☐ _____
- ☐ _____
- ☐ _____
- ☐ _____

Notes:_____

_____

_____

_____

TIME	APPOINTMENTS

HIGHLIGHT OF THE DAY

EXPENSES

Gas: _____

Meals: _____

Mileage: _____

Other: _____

_____

 **success starters**

Friday

Prospecting Tasks

☐ _____
☐ _____
☐ _____
☐ _____
☐ _____
☐ _____

Marketing Tasks

☐ _____
☐ _____
☐ _____
☐ _____
☐ _____
☐ _____

Notes:_____
_____
_____
_____

TIME	APPOINTMENTS

HIGHLIGHT OF THE DAY

EXPENSES

Gas: _____
Meals: _____
Mileage: _____
Other: _____
_____

 **live and learn**

A value proposition is a major factor in determining whether people will bother reading about your services. Work with a partner to develop your value proposition.

Saturday

Prospecting Tasks

☐ _____
☐ _____
☐ _____
☐ _____
☐ _____
☐ _____

Marketing Tasks

☐ _____
☐ _____
☐ _____
☐ _____
☐ _____
☐ _____

Notes:_____
_____
_____
_____

TIME   APPOINTMENTS

HIGHLIGHT OF THE DAY

EXPENSES

Gas: _____

Meals: _____

Mileage: _____

Other: _____

_____

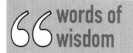

words of wisdom

"Where there is no struggle, there is no strength."
—Oprah Winfrey, American media proprietor, talk show host, actress, producer, and philanthropist

Sunday

Prospecting Tasks

☐ _____
☐ _____
☐ _____
☐ _____
☐ _____
☐ _____

Marketing Tasks

☐ _____
☐ _____
☐ _____
☐ _____
☐ _____
☐ _____

Notes: _____
_____
_____
_____

TIME	APPOINTMENTS

HIGHLIGHT OF THE DAY

EXPENSES

Gas: _____

Meals: _____

Mileage: _____

Other: _____

_____

Weekly Wrap-Up

GOALS:

☐ Met

☐ Exceeded

☐ Maybe Next Week

Highlight of the Week: _____
_____
_____

Prospecting Notes: _____
_____
_____

Marketing Notes: _____
_____
_____

Networking Notes: _____
_____
_____

Professional Development Notes: _____
_____
_____

THOUGHTS ABOUT THE WEEK

Week 12

Dates: _____

Goals: _____

Monday

Prospecting Tasks

- ☐ _____
- ☐ _____
- ☐ _____
- ☐ _____
- ☐ _____
- ☐ _____

Marketing Tasks

- ☐ _____
- ☐ _____
- ☐ _____
- ☐ _____
- ☐ _____
- ☐ _____

Notes: _____

_____

_____

_____

TIME	APPOINTMENTS

HIGHLIGHT OF THE DAY

EXPENSES

Gas: _____

Meals: _____

Mileage: _____

Other: _____

_____

technology tips

Mobile phones have become commonplace, and are a great way to send text messages that promote your latest listings to your clients, friends, and circle of influence.

Tuesday

Prospecting Tasks

- ☐ _____
- ☐ _____
- ☐ _____
- ☐ _____
- ☐ _____
- ☐ _____

Marketing Tasks

- ☐ _____
- ☐ _____
- ☐ _____
- ☐ _____
- ☐ _____
- ☐ _____

Notes:_____
_____
_____
_____

TIME   APPOINTMENTS

HIGHLIGHT OF THE DAY

EXPENSES

Gas: _____

Meals: _____

Mileage: _____

Other: _____

_____

prospecting pointers

If you hear, "No, I am not interested," acknowledge this and move on. Focus on finding customers that want and need your help today.

Wednesday

Prospecting Tasks

- ☐ _____
- ☐ _____
- ☐ _____
- ☐ _____
- ☐ _____
- ☐ _____

Marketing Tasks

- ☐ _____
- ☐ _____
- ☐ _____
- ☐ _____
- ☐ _____
- ☐ _____

Notes:_____
_____
_____
_____

TIME   APPOINTMENTS

HIGHLIGHT OF THE DAY

EXPENSES

Gas: _____

Meals: _____

Mileage: _____

Other: _____

_____

 **marketing matters**

Real estate experts often get free television or radio time when participating in an interview. Establish relationships that will lead to free publicity.

Thursday

Prospecting Tasks

- [ ] _____
- [ ] _____
- [ ] _____
- [ ] _____
- [ ] _____
- [ ] _____

Marketing Tasks

- [ ] _____
- [ ] _____
- [ ] _____
- [ ] _____
- [ ] _____
- [ ] _____

Notes:_____

_____

_____

_____

TIME   APPOINTMENTS

HIGHLIGHT OF THE DAY

EXPENSES

Gas: _____

Meals: _____

Mileage: _____

Other: _____

_____

**success starters**

Send emails or make phone calls to past clients to solicit online reviews.

Friday

Prospecting Tasks

- ☐ _____
- ☐ _____
- ☐ _____
- ☐ _____
- ☐ _____
- ☐ _____

Marketing Tasks

- ☐ _____
- ☐ _____
- ☐ _____
- ☐ _____
- ☐ _____
- ☐ _____

Notes: _____
_____
_____
_____

TIME   APPOINTMENTS

HIGHLIGHT OF THE DAY

EXPENSES

Gas: _____

Meals: _____

Mileage: _____

Other: _____

_____

Books on tape are a great way to educate yourself while driving around town. You can even download audio books onto your smartphone and listen between appointments or meetings.

Saturday

Prospecting Tasks

- ☐ _____
- ☐ _____
- ☐ _____
- ☐ _____
- ☐ _____
- ☐ _____

Marketing Tasks

- ☐ _____
- ☐ _____
- ☐ _____
- ☐ _____
- ☐ _____
- ☐ _____

Notes:_____

_____

_____

_____

TIME   APPOINTMENTS

HIGHLIGHT OF THE DAY

EXPENSES

Gas: _____

Meals: _____

Mileage: _____

Other: _____

_____

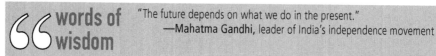

Sunday

Prospecting Tasks

☐ _____
☐ _____
☐ _____
☐ _____
☐ _____
☐ _____

Marketing Tasks

☐ _____
☐ _____
☐ _____
☐ _____
☐ _____
☐ _____

Notes: _____

_____

_____

_____

TIME	APPOINTMENTS

HIGHLIGHT OF THE DAY

EXPENSES

Gas: _____

Meals: _____

Mileage: _____

Other: _____

_____

Weekly Wrap-Up

GOALS:

- ☐ Met
- ☐ Exceeded
- ☐ Maybe Next Week

Highlight of the Week: _____
_____
_____

Prospecting Notes: _____
_____
_____

Marketing Notes: _____
_____
_____

Networking Notes: _____
_____
_____

Professional Development Notes: _____
_____
_____

THOUGHTS ABOUT THE WEEK

Week 13

Dates: _____

Goals: _____

Monday

Prospecting Tasks

- ☐ _____
- ☐ _____
- ☐ _____
- ☐ _____
- ☐ _____
- ☐

Marketing Tasks

- ☐ _____
- ☐ _____
- ☐ _____
- ☐ _____
- ☐ _____
- ☐ _____

Notes: _____
_____
_____
_____

TIME	APPOINTMENTS

HIGHLIGHT OF THE DAY

EXPENSES

Gas: _____

Meals: _____

Mileage: _____

Other: _____

_____

technology tips

A smartphone is not just a telephone; it is a digital assistant. When you use it well, it can increase productivity ten-fold.

Tuesday

Prospecting Tasks

- ☐ _____
- ☐ _____
- ☐ _____
- ☐ _____
- ☐ _____
- ☐ _____

Marketing Tasks

- ☐ _____
- ☐ _____
- ☐ _____
- ☐ _____
- ☐ _____
- ☐ _____

Notes:_____
_____
_____
_____

TIME   APPOINTMENTS

HIGHLIGHT OF THE DAY

EXPENSES

Gas: _____

Meals: _____

Mileage: _____

Other: _____

_____

prospecting pointers Try to avoid sounding overly enthusiastic and unusually friendly. Present facts about your services without any overt persuasion.

Wednesday

Prospecting Tasks

☐ _____
☐ _____
☐ _____
☐ _____
☐ _____
☐ _____

Marketing Tasks

☐ _____
☐ _____
☐ _____
☐ _____
☐ _____
☐ _____

Notes:_____
_____
_____
_____
_____

TIME   APPOINTMENTS

HIGHLIGHT OF THE DAY

EXPENSES

Gas: _____

Meals: _____

Mileage: _____

Other: _____

_____

Bus stop and shopping cart advertising will assure that everyone knows your name. It is a subtle way to increase brand recognition.

Thursday

Prospecting Tasks

- ☐ _____
- ☐ _____
- ☐ _____
- ☐ _____
- ☐ _____
- ☐ _____

Marketing Tasks

- ☐ _____
- ☐ _____
- ☐ _____
- ☐ _____
- ☐ _____
- ☐ _____

Notes:_____

_____

_____

_____

TIME   APPOINTMENTS

HIGHLIGHT OF THE DAY

EXPENSES

Gas: _____

Meals: _____

Mileage: _____

Other: _____

_____

Review any blog posts that you have written. Work to optimize them by using strong keywords that will help these posts rank better on search engines.

Friday

Prospecting Tasks

☐ _____
☐ _____
☐ _____
☐ _____
☐ _____
☐ _____

Marketing Tasks

☐ _____
☐ _____
☐ _____
☐ _____
☐ _____
☐ _____

Notes:_____
_____
_____
_____

TIME **APPOINTMENTS**

HIGHLIGHT OF THE DAY

EXPENSES

Gas: _____
Meals: _____
Mileage: _____
Other: _____
_____

 **live and learn**

Teleconferences and webinars are available everywhere you look. Sign up for these free educational opportunities; they'll motivate you and provide new ideas for building your business.

Saturday

Prospecting Tasks

☐ _____
☐ _____
☐ _____
☐ _____
☐ _____
☐ _____

Marketing Tasks

☐ _____
☐ _____
☐ _____
☐ _____
☐ _____
☐ _____

Notes:_____
_____
_____
_____

TIME   **APPOINTMENTS**

HIGHLIGHT OF THE DAY

EXPENSES

Gas: _____

Meals: _____

Mileage: _____

Other: _____

_____

words of wisdom

"Do one thing every day that scares you."
—Eleanor Roosevelt, longest-serving
First Lady of the United States

Sunday

Prospecting Tasks

- ☐ _____
- ☐ _____
- ☐ _____
- ☐ _____
- ☐ _____
- ☐ _____

Marketing Tasks

- ☐ _____
- ☐ _____
- ☐ _____
- ☐ _____
- ☐ _____
- ☐ _____

Notes:_____

_____

_____

_____

TIME   APPOINTMENTS

HIGHLIGHT OF THE DAY

EXPENSES

Gas: _____

Meals: _____

Mileage: _____

Other: _____

_____

Weekly Wrap-Up

WEEKLY RATING

GOALS:

☐ Met

☐ Exceeded

☐ Maybe Next Week

Highlight of the Week: _____

_____

_____

Prospecting Notes: _____

_____

_____

Marketing Notes: _____

_____

_____

Networking Notes: _____

_____

_____

Professional Development Notes: _____

_____

_____

THOUGHTS ABOUT THE WEEK

Week 14

Dates: _____

Goals: _____

Monday

Prospecting Tasks

- ☐ _____
- ☐ _____
- ☐ _____
- ☐ _____
- ☐ _____
- ☐ _____

Marketing Tasks

- ☐ _____
- ☐ _____
- ☐ _____
- ☐ _____
- ☐ _____
- ☐ _____

Notes:_____

_____

_____

_____

TIME   APPOINTMENTS

HIGHLIGHT OF THE DAY

EXPENSES

Gas: _____

Meals: _____

Mileage: _____

Other: _____

_____

technology tips

Many smartphone users send text messages more often than placing calls. Consider how SMS marketing can be added to your marketing plan.

Tuesday

Prospecting Tasks

- ☐ _____
- ☐ _____
- ☐ _____
- ☐ _____
- ☐ _____
- ☐ _____

Marketing Tasks

- ☐ _____
- ☐ _____
- ☐ _____
- ☐ _____
- ☐ _____
- ☐ _____

Notes:_____
_____
_____
_____

TIME   APPOINTMENTS

HIGHLIGHT OF THE DAY

EXPENSES

Gas: _____

Meals: _____

Mileage: _____

Other: _____

_____

Wednesday

Prospecting Tasks

☐ _____
☐ _____
☐ _____
☐ _____
☐ _____
☐ _____

Marketing Tasks

☐ _____
☐ _____
☐ _____
☐ _____
☐ _____
☐ _____

Notes:_____
_____
_____
_____

TIME   APPOINTMENTS

HIGHLIGHT OF THE DAY

EXPENSES

Gas: _____

Meals: _____

Mileage: _____

Other: _____

_____

 **marketing matters**

According to a 2013 survey, 8 out of 10 say they trust online reviews as much as personal recommendations. Ask past clients to review your services on popular sites such as Yelp or Google.

Thursday

Prospecting Tasks

- ☐ _____
- ☐ _____
- ☐ _____
- ☐ _____
- ☐ _____
- ☐ _____

Marketing Tasks

- ☐ _____
- ☐ _____
- ☐ _____
- ☐ _____
- ☐ _____
- ☐ _____

Notes: _____
_____
_____
_____

TIME   **APPOINTMENTS**

HIGHLIGHT OF THE DAY

EXPENSES

Gas: _____

Meals: _____

Mileage: _____

Other: _____

_____

Write and mail five personal notes per week. Thoughtful notes to people that you know are a great way to keep in touch and foster deeper relationships.

Friday

Prospecting Tasks

- ☐ _____
- ☐ _____
- ☐ _____
- ☐ _____
- ☐ _____
- ☐ _____

Marketing Tasks

- ☐ _____
- ☐ _____
- ☐ _____
- ☐ _____
- ☐ _____
- ☐ _____

Notes:_____

_____

_____

_____

TIME   APPOINTMENTS

HIGHLIGHT OF THE DAY

EXPENSES

Gas:_____

Meals:_____

Mileage:_____

Other:_____

_____

 **live and learn**

Have tools to network with you at all times. These include a name badge, business cards, brochures, and information about other professionals whom you can refer.

Saturday

Prospecting Tasks

- ☐ _____
- ☐ _____
- ☐ _____
- ☐ _____
- ☐ _____
- ☐ _____

Marketing Tasks

- ☐ _____
- ☐ _____
- ☐ _____
- ☐ _____
- ☐ _____
- ☐ _____

Notes:_____

_____

_____

_____

TIME   APPOINTMENTS

HIGHLIGHT OF THE DAY

EXPENSES

Gas: _____

Meals: _____

Mileage: _____

Other: _____

_____

Sunday

Prospecting Tasks

- ☐ _____
- ☐ _____
- ☐ _____
- ☐ _____
- ☐ _____
- ☐ _____

Marketing Tasks

- ☐ _____
- ☐ _____
- ☐ _____
- ☐ _____
- ☐ _____
- ☐ _____

Notes:_____

_____

_____

_____

TIME   **APPOINTMENTS**

HIGHLIGHT OF THE DAY

EXPENSES

Gas: _____

Meals: _____

Mileage: _____

Other: _____

_____

Weekly Wrap-Up

GOALS:

- ☐ Met
- ☐ Exceeded
- ☐ Maybe Next Week

Highlight of the Week: _____

_____

_____

Prospecting Notes: _____

_____

_____

Marketing Notes: _____

_____

_____

Networking Notes: _____

_____

_____

Professional Development Notes: _____

_____

_____

THOUGHTS ABOUT THE WEEK

Week 15

Dates: _____

Goals: _____

Monday

Prospecting Tasks

- ☐ _____
- ☐ _____
- ☐ _____
- ☐ _____
- ☐ _____
- ☐ _____

Marketing Tasks

- ☐ _____
- ☐ _____
- ☐ _____
- ☐ _____
- ☐ _____
- ☐ _____

Notes: _____

_____

_____

_____

TIME	APPOINTMENTS

HIGHLIGHT OF THE DAY

EXPENSES

Gas: _____

Meals: _____

Mileage: _____

Other: _____

_____

technology tips

By connecting with industry players to display your services on their desktop, you can boost your presence and provide top of mind awareness.

Tuesday

Prospecting Tasks

☐ _____
☐ _____
☐ _____
☐ _____
☐ _____
☐ _____

Marketing Tasks

☐ _____
☐ _____
☐ _____
☐ _____
☐ _____
☐ _____

Notes: _____
_____
_____
_____

TIME   APPOINTMENTS

HIGHLIGHT OF THE DAY

EXPENSES

Gas: _____
Meals: _____
Mileage: _____
Other: _____
_____

prospecting pointers

Record your calls and listen to the way you sound. This will help you in altering your conversation to convince prospects better.

Wednesday

Prospecting Tasks

☐ _____
☐ _____
☐ _____
☐ _____
☐ _____
☐ _____

Marketing Tasks

☐ _____
☐ _____
☐ _____
☐ _____
☐ _____
☐ _____

Notes:_____
_____
_____
_____

TIME   APPOINTMENTS

HIGHLIGHT OF THE DAY

EXPENSES

Gas: _____

Meals: _____

Mileage: _____

Other: _____

_____

 **marketing matters**

Make use of social media channels like Facebook to unleash a wave of campaigns that target thousands of net users; include seller and buyer marketing in your bag of tricks!

Thursday

Prospecting Tasks

☐ _____
☐ _____
☐ _____
☐ _____
☐ _____
☐ _____

Marketing Tasks

☐ _____
☐ _____
☐ _____
☐ _____
☐ _____
☐ _____

Notes: _____
_____
_____
_____

TIME   **APPOINTMENTS**

HIGHLIGHT OF THE DAY

EXPENSES

Gas: _____

Meals: _____

Mileage: _____

Other: _____

_____

success starters

Contact any clients currently under contract and ask them if they know anyone that might be interested in buying or selling now or in the near future.

Friday

Prospecting Tasks

- [ ] _____
- [ ] _____
- [ ] _____
- [ ] _____
- [ ] _____
- [ ] _____

Marketing Tasks

- [ ] _____
- [ ] _____
- [ ] _____
- [ ] _____
- [ ] _____
- [ ] _____

Notes:_____

_____

_____

_____

TIME   APPOINTMENTS

HIGHLIGHT OF THE DAY

EXPENSES

Gas: _____

Meals: _____

Mileage: _____

Other: _____

_____

live and learn

When you volunteer to participate on committees at your local Realtor® association, you create goodwill and get opportunities to network with top-notch agents in your area.

Saturday

Prospecting Tasks

- ☐ _____
- ☐ _____
- ☐ _____
- ☐ _____
- ☐ _____
- ☐ _____

Marketing Tasks

- ☐ _____
- ☐ _____
- ☐ _____
- ☐ _____
- ☐ _____
- ☐ _____

Notes:_____

_____

_____

_____

TIME   APPOINTMENTS

HIGHLIGHT OF THE DAY

EXPENSES

Gas: _____

Meals: _____

Mileage: _____

Other: _____

_____

words of wisdom

"Be a yardstick of quality. Some people aren't used to an environment where excellence is expected."
—**Steve Jobs**, entrepreneur and co-founder of Apple, Inc.

Sunday

Prospecting Tasks

☐ _____
☐ _____
☐ _____
☐ _____
☐ _____
☐ _____

Marketing Tasks

☐ _____
☐ _____
☐ _____
☐ _____
☐ _____
☐ _____

Notes: _____

_____

_____

_____

TIME	APPOINTMENTS

HIGHLIGHT OF THE DAY

EXPENSES

Gas: _____

Meals: _____

Mileage: _____

Other: _____

_____

Weekly Wrap-Up

WEEKLY RATING

GOALS:

☐ Met

☐ Exceeded

☐ Maybe Next Week

Highlight of the Week: _____

_____

_____

Prospecting Notes: _____

_____

_____

Marketing Notes: _____

_____

_____

Networking Notes: _____

_____

_____

Professional Development Notes: _____

_____

_____

THOUGHTS ABOUT THE WEEK

Week 16

Dates: _____

Goals: _____

Monday

Prospecting Tasks

- ☐ _____
- ☐ _____
- ☐ _____
- ☐ _____
- ☐ _____
- ☐ _____

Marketing Tasks

- ☐ _____
- ☐ _____
- ☐ _____
- ☐ _____
- ☐ _____
- ☐ _____

Notes: _____

_____

_____

_____

TIME	APPOINTMENTS

HIGHLIGHT OF THE DAY

EXPENSES

Gas: _____

Meals: _____

Mileage: _____

Other: _____

_____

technology tips

Seek out companies offering digital TV and cable advertising services and take advantage of this technology in advertising your products.

Tuesday

Prospecting Tasks

- ☐ _____
- ☐ _____
- ☐ _____
- ☐ _____
- ☐ _____
- ☐ _____

Marketing Tasks

- ☐ _____
- ☐ _____
- ☐ _____
- ☐ _____
- ☐ _____
- ☐ _____

Notes:_____

_____

_____

_____

TIME   APPOINTMENTS

HIGHLIGHT OF THE DAY

EXPENSES

Gas: _____

Meals: _____

Mileage: _____

Other: _____

_____

prospecting pointers

Make sure that you converse neutrally and do not seem overly aggressive in seeking an appointment. Neutral conversations create grounds for follow-up calls.

Wednesday

Prospecting Tasks

☐ _____
☐ _____
☐ _____
☐ _____
☐ _____
☐ _____

Marketing Tasks

☐ _____
☐ _____
☐ _____
☐ _____
☐ _____
☐ _____

Notes:_____
_____
_____
_____

TIME   APPOINTMENTS

HIGHLIGHT OF THE DAY

EXPENSES

Gas: _____
Meals: _____
Mileage: _____
Other: _____
_____

 **marketing matters**

Build a simple and easy-to-navigate personal website. A website that is visually appealing and easy to use will lead to a lower bounce rate and increased lead conversion.

Thursday

Prospecting Tasks

- ☐ _____
- ☐ _____
- ☐ _____
- ☐ _____
- ☐ _____
- ☐ _____

Marketing Tasks

- ☐ _____
- ☐ _____
- ☐ _____
- ☐ _____
- ☐ _____
- ☐ _____

Notes:_____

_____

_____

_____

TIME	APPOINTMENTS

HIGHLIGHT OF THE DAY

EXPENSES

Gas: _____

Meals: _____

Mileage: _____

Other: _____

_____

 **success starters**

Have a look at your print marketing materials. Is the information up to date? If not, it may be time to make a few changes.

Friday

Prospecting Tasks

☐ _____
☐ _____
☐ _____
☐ _____
☐ _____
☐ _____

Marketing Tasks

☐ _____
☐ _____
☐ _____
☐ _____
☐ _____
☐ _____

Notes: _____
_____
_____
_____

TIME   APPOINTMENTS

HIGHLIGHT OF THE DAY

EXPENSES

Gas: _____

Meals: _____

Mileage: _____

Other: _____

_____

 **live and learn**

Take time to conduct a SWOT analysis of your business. When you identify strengths, weaknesses, opportunities, and threats, you see where improvement is needed.

Saturday

Prospecting Tasks

☐ _____
☐ _____
☐ _____
☐ _____
☐ _____
☐ _____

Marketing Tasks

☐ _____
☐ _____
☐ _____
☐ _____
☐ _____
☐ _____

Notes:_____
_____
_____
_____

TIME	APPOINTMENTS

HIGHLIGHT OF THE DAY

EXPENSES

Gas: _____
Meals: _____
Mileage: _____
Other: _____
_____

"The way I see it, if you want the rainbow, you gotta put up with the rain."
—Dolly Parton, country music singer-songwriter, actress, author, and philanthropist

Sunday

Prospecting Tasks

- ☐ _____
- ☐ _____
- ☐ _____
- ☐ _____
- ☐ _____
- ☐ _____

Marketing Tasks

- ☐ _____
- ☐ _____
- ☐ _____
- ☐ _____
- ☐ _____
- ☐ _____

Notes:_____
_____
_____
_____

TIME   APPOINTMENTS

HIGHLIGHT OF THE DAY

EXPENSES

Gas: _____

Meals: _____

Mileage: _____

Other: _____

_____

Weekly Wrap-Up

GOALS:

☐ Met

☐ Exceeded

☐ Maybe Next Week

Highlight of the Week: _____

_____

_____

Prospecting Notes: _____

_____

_____

Marketing Notes: _____

_____

_____

Networking Notes: _____

_____

_____

Professional Development Notes: _____

_____

_____

THOUGHTS ABOUT THE WEEK

Week 17

Dates: _____

Goals: _____

Monday

Prospecting Tasks

- ☐ _____
- ☐ _____
- ☐ _____
- ☐ _____
- ☐ _____
- ☐ _____

Marketing Tasks

- ☐ _____
- ☐ _____
- ☐ _____
- ☐ _____
- ☐ _____
- ☐ _____

Notes: _____
_____
_____
_____

TIME   APPOINTMENTS

HIGHLIGHT OF THE DAY

EXPENSES

Gas: _____

Meals: _____

Mileage: _____

Other: _____

_____

technology tips

Incorporating your company's services into a self-contained program or app can serve to enhance the brand image of your company.

Tuesday

Prospecting Tasks

☐ _____
☐ _____
☐ _____
☐ _____
☐ _____
☐ _____

Marketing Tasks

☐ _____
☐ _____
☐ _____
☐ _____
☐ _____
☐ _____

Notes: _____
_____
_____
_____

TIME	APPOINTMENTS

HIGHLIGHT OF THE DAY

EXPENSES

Gas: _____

Meals: _____

Mileage: _____

Other: _____

_____

prospecting pointers — In the first few minutes of your conversation, you need to differentiate between low probability and high probability prospects, so that you can market your services effectively.

Wednesday

Prospecting Tasks

- [ ] _____
- [ ] _____
- [ ] _____
- [ ] _____
- [ ] _____
- [ ] _____

Marketing Tasks

- [ ] _____
- [ ] _____
- [ ] _____
- [ ] _____
- [ ] _____
- [ ] _____

Notes:_____

_____

_____

_____

TIME   APPOINTMENTS

HIGHLIGHT OF THE DAY

EXPENSES

Gas: _____

Meals: _____

Mileage: _____

Other: _____

_____

 **marketing matters**

Create and upload instructional videos to sites such as YouTube and Vimeo; include information about the ins and outs of the home buying and home selling in your videos.

Thursday

Prospecting Tasks

☐ _____
☐ _____
☐ _____
☐ _____
☐ _____
☐ _____

Marketing Tasks

☐ _____
☐ _____
☐ _____
☐ _____
☐ _____
☐ _____

Notes:_____
_____
_____
_____

TIME   APPOINTMENTS

HIGHLIGHT OF THE DAY

EXPENSES

Gas: _____

Meals: _____

Mileage: _____

Other: _____

_____

success starters

Providing something of value is a great way to generate new business. Offer a free ebook or a free educational course in order to generate leads in your niche market.

Friday

Prospecting Tasks

- ☐ _____
- ☐ _____
- ☐ _____
- ☐ _____
- ☐ _____
- ☐ _____

Marketing Tasks

- ☐ _____
- ☐ _____
- ☐ _____
- ☐ _____
- ☐ _____
- ☐ _____

Notes:_____

_____

_____

_____

TIME   APPOINTMENTS

HIGHLIGHT OF THE DAY

EXPENSES

Gas: _____

Meals: _____

Mileage: _____

Other: _____

_____

 **live and learn**

When networking, act like a host and not a guest. At local events, volunteer to greet people. If you see people seated, introduce yourself and ask whether they would like to meet others.

Saturday

Prospecting Tasks

- ☐ _____
- ☐ _____
- ☐ _____
- ☐ _____
- ☐ _____
- ☐ _____

Marketing Tasks

- ☐ _____
- ☐ _____
- ☐ _____
- ☐ _____
- ☐ _____
- ☐ _____

Notes: _____
_____
_____
_____

TIME	APPOINTMENTS

HIGHLIGHT OF THE DAY

EXPENSES

Gas: _____

Meals: _____

Mileage: _____

Other: _____

_____

words of wisdom

"The foundation stones for a balanced success are honesty, character, integrity, faith, love, and loyalty."
—Zig Ziglar, author, salesman, and motivational speaker

Sunday

Prospecting Tasks

- ☐ _____
- ☐ _____
- ☐ _____
- ☐ _____
- ☐ _____
- ☐ _____

Marketing Tasks

- ☐ _____
- ☐ _____
- ☐ _____
- ☐ _____
- ☐ _____
- ☐ _____

Notes:_____
_____
_____
_____

TIME   **APPOINTMENTS**

HIGHLIGHT OF THE DAY

EXPENSES

Gas: _____

Meals: _____

Mileage: _____

Other: _____

_____

Weekly Wrap-Up

GOALS:

☐ Met

☐ Exceeded

☐ Maybe Next Week

Highlight of the Week: _____

_____

_____

Prospecting Notes: _____

_____

_____

Marketing Notes: _____

_____

_____

Networking Notes: _____

_____

_____

Professional Development Notes: _____

_____

_____

THOUGHTS ABOUT THE WEEK

Week 18

Dates: _____

Goals: _____

Monday

Prospecting Tasks

- ☐ _____
- ☐ _____
- ☐ _____
- ☐ _____
- ☐ _____
- ☐ _____

Marketing Tasks

- ☐ _____
- ☐ _____
- ☐ _____
- ☐ _____
- ☐ _____
- ☐ _____

Notes:_____

_____

_____

_____

TIME	APPOINTMENTS

HIGHLIGHT OF THE DAY

EXPENSES

Gas: _____

Meals: _____

Mileage: _____

Other: _____

_____

Tuesday

Prospecting Tasks

- ☐ _____
- ☐ _____
- ☐ _____
- ☐ _____
- ☐ _____
- ☐ _____

Marketing Tasks

- ☐ _____
- ☐ _____
- ☐ _____
- ☐ _____
- ☐ _____
- ☐ _____

Notes: _____
_____
_____
_____

TIME   APPOINTMENTS

HIGHLIGHT OF THE DAY

EXPENSES

Gas: _____

Meals: _____

Mileage: _____

Other: _____

_____

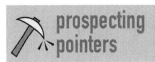

Wednesday

Prospecting Tasks

☐ _____
☐ _____
☐ _____
☐ _____
☐ _____
☐ _____

Marketing Tasks

☐ _____
☐ _____
☐ _____
☐ _____
☐ _____
☐ _____

Notes:_____
_____
_____
_____

TIME   APPOINTMENTS

HIGHLIGHT OF THE DAY

EXPENSES

Gas: _____
Meals: _____
Mileage: _____
Other: _____
_____

**marketing matters**

Enter into partnerships with market leaders of local businesses; this will give you a way to advertise your services on new platforms.

Thursday

Prospecting Tasks

☐ _____
☐ _____
☐ _____
☐ _____
☐ _____
☐ _____

Marketing Tasks

☐ _____
☐ _____
☐ _____
☐ _____
☐ _____
☐ _____

Notes: _____
_____
_____
_____

TIME   **APPOINTMENTS**

HIGHLIGHT OF THE DAY

EXPENSES

Gas: _____

Meals: _____

Mileage: _____

Other: _____

_____

success starters

Join an online networking community, such as LinkedIn or ActiveRain. Read and comment on blog posts in order to establish relationships and learn at the same time.

Friday

Prospecting Tasks

☐ _____
☐ _____
☐ _____
☐ _____
☐ _____
☐ _____

Marketing Tasks

☐ _____
☐ _____
☐ _____
☐ _____
☐ _____
☐ _____

Notes:_____
_____
_____
_____

TIME   APPOINTMENTS

HIGHLIGHT OF THE DAY

EXPENSES

Gas: _____

Meals: _____

Mileage: _____

Other: _____

_____

live and learn

The National Association of Realtors® provides a wide range of programs and services that assist members in increasing skills, proficiency, and knowledge.

Saturday

Prospecting Tasks

- ☐ _____
- ☐ _____
- ☐ _____
- ☐ _____
- ☐ _____
- ☐ _____

Marketing Tasks

- ☐ _____
- ☐ _____
- ☐ _____
- ☐ _____
- ☐ _____
- ☐ _____

Notes: _____

_____

_____

_____

TIME   APPOINTMENTS

HIGHLIGHT OF THE DAY

EXPENSES

Gas: _____

Meals: _____

Mileage: _____

Other: _____

_____

words of wisdom

"Perseverance is failing 19 times and succeeding the 20th."
—Julie Andrews, film and stage actress,
author, director, and dancer

Sunday

Prospecting Tasks

☐ _____
☐ _____
☐ _____
☐ _____
☐ _____
☐ _____

Marketing Tasks

☐ _____
☐ _____
☐ _____
☐ _____
☐ _____
☐ _____

Notes:_____
_____
_____
_____

TIME	APPOINTMENTS

HIGHLIGHT OF THE DAY

EXPENSES

Gas: _____
Meals: _____
Mileage: _____
Other: _____
_____

Weekly Wrap-Up

GOALS:

- ☐ Met
- ☐ Exceeded
- ☐ Maybe Next Week

Highlight of the Week: _____

_____

_____

Prospecting Notes: _____

_____

_____

Marketing Notes: _____

_____

_____

Networking Notes: _____

_____

_____

Professional Development Notes: _____

_____

_____

THOUGHTS ABOUT THE WEEK

Week 19

Dates: _____

Goals: _____

Monday

Prospecting Tasks

- ☐ _____
- ☐ _____
- ☐ _____
- ☐ _____
- ☐ _____
- ☐ _____

Marketing Tasks

- ☐ _____
- ☐ _____
- ☐ _____
- ☐ _____
- ☐ _____
- ☐ _____

Notes: _____

_____

_____

_____

TIME	APPOINTMENTS

HIGHLIGHT OF THE DAY

EXPENSES

Gas: _____

Meals: _____

Mileage: _____

Other: _____

_____

Tuesday

Prospecting Tasks

- ☐ _____
- ☐ _____
- ☐ _____
- ☐ _____
- ☐ _____
- ☐ _____

Marketing Tasks

- ☐ _____
- ☐ _____
- ☐ _____
- ☐ _____
- ☐ _____
- ☐ _____

Notes: _____
_____
_____
_____

TIME	APPOINTMENTS

HIGHLIGHT OF THE DAY

EXPENSES

Gas: _____

Meals: _____

Mileage: _____

Other: _____

_____

Wednesday

Prospecting Tasks

- ☐ _____
- ☐ _____
- ☐ _____
- ☐ _____
- ☐ _____
- ☐ _____

Marketing Tasks

- ☐ _____
- ☐ _____
- ☐ _____
- ☐ _____
- ☐ _____
- ☐ _____

Notes:_____

_____

_____

_____

TIME   APPOINTMENTS

HIGHLIGHT OF THE DAY

EXPENSES

Gas: _____

Meals: _____

Mileage: _____

Other: _____

_____

marketing matters

Online lead generation platforms provide a full range of tools, which you can leverage to increase your market share. Program subscriptions could reap many buyer leads.

Thursday

Prospecting Tasks

- ☐ _____
- ☐ _____
- ☐ _____
- ☐ _____
- ☐ _____
- ☐ _____

Marketing Tasks

- ☐ _____
- ☐ _____
- ☐ _____
- ☐ _____
- ☐ _____
- ☐ _____

Notes:_____

_____

_____

_____

TIME   APPOINTMENTS

HIGHLIGHT OF THE DAY

EXPENSES

Gas: _____

Meals: _____

Mileage: _____

Other: _____

_____

success starters

Check your email signature line. Does it include your real estate license number, phone number, and a link to your website? It may be time to update your information.

Friday

Prospecting Tasks

- ☐ _____
- ☐ _____
- ☐ _____
- ☐ _____
- ☐ _____
- ☐ _____

Marketing Tasks

- ☐ _____
- ☐ _____
- ☐ _____
- ☐ _____
- ☐ _____
- ☐ _____

Notes: _____

_____

_____

_____

TIME   APPOINTMENTS

HIGHLIGHT OF THE DAY

EXPENSES

Gas: _____

Meals: _____

Mileage: _____

Other: _____

_____

 **live and learn**

Many people love to read because books offer an escape from everyday activities. Investigate books that will invigorate your spirit and bring new ideas to your business platform.

Saturday

Prospecting Tasks

☐ _____
☐ _____
☐ _____
☐ _____
☐ _____
☐ _____

Marketing Tasks

☐ _____
☐ _____
☐ _____
☐ _____
☐ _____
☐ _____

Notes: _____
_____
_____
_____

TIME   APPOINTMENTS

HIGHLIGHT OF THE DAY

EXPENSES

Gas: _____

Meals: _____

Mileage: _____

Other: _____

_____

Sunday

Prospecting Tasks

- ☐ _____
- ☐ _____
- ☐ _____
- ☐ _____
- ☐ _____
- ☐ _____

Marketing Tasks

- ☐ _____
- ☐ _____
- ☐ _____
- ☐ _____
- ☐ _____
- ☐ _____

Notes: _____

_____

_____

_____

TIME	APPOINTMENTS

HIGHLIGHT OF THE DAY

EXPENSES

Gas: _____

Meals: _____

Mileage: _____

Other: _____

_____

Weekly Wrap-Up

GOALS:

- ☐ Met
- ☐ Exceeded
- ☐ Maybe Next Week

Highlight of the Week: _____

_____

_____

Prospecting Notes: _____

_____

_____

Marketing Notes: _____

_____

_____

Networking Notes: _____

_____

_____

Professional Development Notes: _____

_____

_____

THOUGHTS ABOUT THE WEEK

Week 20

Dates: _____

Goals: _____

Monday

Prospecting Tasks

- [ ] _____
- [ ] _____
- [ ] _____
- [ ] _____
- [ ] _____
- [ ] _____

Marketing Tasks

- [ ] _____
- [ ] _____
- [ ] _____
- [ ] _____
- [ ] _____
- [ ] _____

Notes: _____
_____
_____
_____

TIME	APPOINTMENTS

HIGHLIGHT OF THE DAY

EXPENSES

Gas: _____

Meals: _____

Mileage: _____

Other: _____

_____

Tuesday

Prospecting Tasks

- ☐ _____
- ☐ _____
- ☐ _____
- ☐ _____
- ☐ _____
- ☐ _____

Marketing Tasks

- ☐ _____
- ☐ _____
- ☐ _____
- ☐ _____
- ☐ _____
- ☐ _____

Notes:_____

_____

_____

_____

TIME   **APPOINTMENTS**

HIGHLIGHT OF THE DAY

EXPENSES

Gas: _____

Meals: _____

Mileage: _____

Other: _____

_____

prospecting pointers — Maintain correct records of prospecting sessions. This will help you analyze and study the way your prospects are converted into clients.

Wednesday

Prospecting Tasks

- ☐ _____
- ☐ _____
- ☐ _____
- ☐ _____
- ☐ _____
- ☐ _____

Marketing Tasks

- ☐ _____
- ☐ _____
- ☐ _____
- ☐ _____
- ☐ _____
- ☐ _____

Notes:_____

_____

_____

_____

TIME **APPOINTMENTS**

HIGHLIGHT OF THE DAY

EXPENSES

Gas: _____

Meals: _____

Mileage: _____

Other: _____

_____

marketing matters

Use public events, such as a street faire or expo, to market your services. Organize raffles and pass out promotional items to secure leads.

Thursday

Prospecting Tasks

- ☐ _____
- ☐ _____
- ☐ _____
- ☐ _____
- ☐ _____
- ☐ _____

Marketing Tasks

- ☐ _____
- ☐ _____
- ☐ _____
- ☐ _____
- ☐ _____
- ☐ _____

Notes:_____

_____

_____

_____

TIME	APPOINTMENTS

HIGHLIGHT OF THE DAY

EXPENSES

Gas: _____

Meals: _____

Mileage: _____

Other: _____

_____

 **success starters**

Use a mobile app, such as Videolicious, in order to make a short video of one of your property listings. Post the video on YouTube and other social media sites.

Friday

Prospecting Tasks

☐ _____
☐ _____
☐ _____
☐ _____
☐ _____
☐ _____

Marketing Tasks

☐ _____
☐ _____
☐ _____
☐ _____
☐ _____
☐ _____

Notes:_____

_____

_____

_____

TIME	APPOINTMENTS

HIGHLIGHT OF THE DAY

EXPENSES

Gas: _____

Meals: _____

Mileage: _____

Other: _____

_____

The DISC assessment is a tool that centers around four different personality traits. Conduct a DISC assessment and identify the real estate activities that will bring you the most success.

Saturday

Prospecting Tasks

- [ ] _____
- [ ] _____
- [ ] _____
- [ ] _____
- [ ] _____
- [ ] _____

Marketing Tasks

- [ ] _____
- [ ] _____
- [ ] _____
- [ ] _____
- [ ] _____
- [ ] _____

Notes:_____

_____

_____

_____

TIME   APPOINTMENTS

HIGHLIGHT OF THE DAY

EXPENSES

Gas: _____

Meals: _____

Mileage: _____

Other: _____

_____

words of wisdom

"Success is a lousy teacher. It seduces smart people into thinking they can't lose."

—**Bill Gates,** business magnate and co-founder of Microsoft Corporation

Sunday

Prospecting Tasks

- [ ] _____
- [ ] _____
- [ ] _____
- [ ] _____
- [ ] _____
- [ ] _____

Marketing Tasks

- [ ] _____
- [ ] _____
- [ ] _____
- [ ] _____
- [ ] _____
- [ ] _____

Notes:_____

_____

_____

_____

TIME   APPOINTMENTS

HIGHLIGHT OF THE DAY

EXPENSES

Gas: _____

Meals: _____

Mileage: _____

Other: _____

_____

Weekly Wrap-Up

GOALS:

☐ Met

☐ Exceeded

☐ Maybe Next Week

Highlight of the Week: _____

_____

_____

Prospecting Notes: _____

_____

_____

Marketing Notes: _____

_____

_____

Networking Notes: _____

_____

_____

Professional Development Notes: _____

_____

_____

THOUGHTS ABOUT THE WEEK

Week 21

Dates: _____

Goals: _____

Monday

Prospecting Tasks

- ☐ _____
- ☐ _____
- ☐ _____
- ☐ _____
- ☐ _____
- ☐ _____

Marketing Tasks

- ☐ _____
- ☐ _____
- ☐ _____
- ☐ _____
- ☐ _____
- ☐ _____

Notes: _____
_____
_____
_____

TIME	APPOINTMENTS

HIGHLIGHT OF THE DAY

EXPENSES

Gas: _____

Meals: _____

Mileage: _____

Other: _____

_____

technology tips

Selecting a good social platform for uploading photos and images can help you in gaining customers and creating visual appeal for your listings at the same time.

Tuesday

Prospecting Tasks

- [ ] _____
- [ ] _____
- [ ] _____
- [ ] _____
- [ ] _____
- [ ] _____

Marketing Tasks

- [ ] _____
- [ ] _____
- [ ] _____
- [ ] _____
- [ ] _____
- [ ] _____

Notes:_____

_____

_____

_____

TIME	APPOINTMENTS

HIGHLIGHT OF THE DAY

EXPENSES

Gas: _____

Meals: _____

Mileage: _____

Other: _____

_____

prospecting pointers

Use your referral network to your advantage and add a chain to the link of existing customers for your real estate services.

Wednesday

Prospecting Tasks

☐ _____
☐ _____
☐ _____
☐ _____
☐ _____
☐ _____

Marketing Tasks

☐ _____
☐ _____
☐ _____
☐ _____
☐ _____
☐ _____

Notes: _____
_____
_____
_____

TIME   **APPOINTMENTS**

HIGHLIGHT OF THE DAY

EXPENSES

Gas: _____

Meals: _____

Mileage: _____

Other: _____

_____

 **marketing matters**

Marketing materials should be easy on the eyes. Use bold and easy-to-read fonts, and remember that less is more.

Thursday

Prospecting Tasks

- ☐ _____
- ☐ _____
- ☐ _____
- ☐ _____
- ☐ _____
- ☐ _____

Marketing Tasks

- ☐ _____
- ☐ _____
- ☐ _____
- ☐ _____
- ☐ _____
- ☐ _____

Notes: _____
_____
_____
_____

TIME	APPOINTMENTS

HIGHLIGHT OF THE DAY

EXPENSES

Gas: _____

Meals: _____

Mileage: _____

Other: _____

_____

 **success starters**

Prepare a personal brochure that includes your value proposition and information about the services that you offer.

Friday

Prospecting Tasks

- ☐ _____
- ☐ _____
- ☐ _____
- ☐ _____
- ☐ _____
- ☐ _____

Marketing Tasks

- ☐ _____
- ☐ _____
- ☐ _____
- ☐ _____
- ☐ _____
- ☐ _____

Notes:_____
_____
_____
_____

TIME   APPOINTMENTS

HIGHLIGHT OF THE DAY

EXPENSES

Gas: _____

Meals: _____

Mileage: _____

Other: _____

_____

 **live and learn**

A good networker has two ears and one mouth and uses them proportionately. Always listen first. After you've learned what another person does, tell what you do. Be brief and informative.

Saturday

Prospecting Tasks

- ☐ _____
- ☐ _____
- ☐ _____
- ☐ _____
- ☐ _____
- ☐ _____

Marketing Tasks

- ☐ _____
- ☐ _____
- ☐ _____
- ☐ _____
- ☐ _____
- ☐ _____

Notes:_____

_____

_____

_____

TIME   **APPOINTMENTS**

HIGHLIGHT OF THE DAY

EXPENSES

Gas: _____

Meals: _____

Mileage: _____

Other: _____

_____

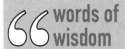
words of wisdom

"Preparation, I have often said, is rightly two-thirds of any venture."
—**Amelia Earhart,** first aviatrix to fly solo across the Atlantic Ocean

Sunday

Prospecting Tasks

☐ _____
☐ _____
☐ _____
☐ _____
☐ _____
☐ _____

Marketing Tasks

☐ _____
☐ _____
☐ _____
☐ _____
☐ _____
☐ _____

Notes: _____
_____
_____
_____

TIME   **APPOINTMENTS**

HIGHLIGHT OF THE DAY

EXPENSES

Gas: _____

Meals: _____

Mileage: _____

Other: _____

_____

Weekly Wrap-Up

GOALS:

- ☐ Met
- ☐ Exceeded
- ☐ Maybe Next Week

Highlight of the Week: _____

_____

_____

Prospecting Notes: _____

_____

_____

Marketing Notes: _____

_____

_____

Networking Notes: _____

_____

_____

Professional Development Notes: _____

_____

_____

THOUGHTS ABOUT THE WEEK

Week 22

Dates: _____

Goals: _____

Monday

Prospecting Tasks

- ☐ _____
- ☐ _____
- ☐ _____
- ☐ _____
- ☐ _____
- ☐ _____

Marketing Tasks

- ☐ _____
- ☐ _____
- ☐ _____
- ☐ _____
- ☐ _____
- ☐ _____

Notes: _____
_____
_____
_____

TIME   APPOINTMENTS

HIGHLIGHT OF THE DAY

EXPENSES

Gas: _____

Meals: _____

Mileage: _____

Other: _____

_____

technology tips

Active social media networking within 140 characters is a challenge, but it's a great way to get your messages out to massive amounts of prospective buyers and sellers.

Tuesday

Prospecting Tasks

- [ ] _____
- [ ] _____
- [ ] _____
- [ ] _____
- [ ] _____
- [ ] _____

Marketing Tasks

- [ ] _____
- [ ] _____
- [ ] _____
- [ ] _____
- [ ] _____
- [ ] _____

Notes:_____

_____

_____

_____

TIME APPOINTMENTS

HIGHLIGHT OF THE DAY

EXPENSES

Gas: _____

Meals: _____

Mileage: _____

Other: _____

_____

 **prospecting pointers**

Ask open-ended questions when speaking with prospects to better understand their exact needs.

Wednesday

Prospecting Tasks

- [ ] _____
- [ ] _____
- [ ] _____
- [ ] _____
- [ ] _____
- [ ] _____

Marketing Tasks

- [ ] _____
- [ ] _____
- [ ] _____
- [ ] _____
- [ ] _____
- [ ] _____

Notes:_____

_____

_____

_____

TIME   APPOINTMENTS

HIGHLIGHT OF THE DAY

EXPENSES

Gas: _____

Meals: _____

Mileage: _____

Other: _____

_____

Use online classifieds to offer your listings and buyer services and to strengthen your company brand.

Thursday

Prospecting Tasks

- ☐ _____
- ☐ _____
- ☐ _____
- ☐ _____
- ☐ _____
- ☐ _____

Marketing Tasks

- ☐ _____
- ☐ _____
- ☐ _____
- ☐ _____
- ☐ _____
- ☐ _____

Notes:_____
_____
_____
_____

TIME	APPOINTMENTS

HIGHLIGHT OF THE DAY

EXPENSES

Gas: _____

Meals: _____

Mileage: _____

Other: _____

_____

Conduct an online search for helpful scripts for real estate agents. Use the scripts in order to hone your real estate skills.

Friday

Prospecting Tasks

☐ _____
☐ _____
☐ _____
☐ _____
☐ _____
☐ _____

Marketing Tasks

☐ _____
☐ _____
☐ _____
☐ _____
☐ _____
☐ _____

Notes: _____
_____
_____
_____

TIME   APPOINTMENTS

HIGHLIGHT OF THE DAY

EXPENSES

Gas: _____

Meals: _____

Mileage: _____

Other: _____

_____

 **live and learn**

Professional development encompasses more than just continuing education courses. Local area knowledge, as well as being current on real estate industry news and trends, is very important.

Saturday

Prospecting Tasks

- ☐ _____
- ☐ _____
- ☐ _____
- ☐ _____
- ☐ _____
- ☐ _____

Marketing Tasks

- ☐ _____
- ☐ _____
- ☐ _____
- ☐ _____
- ☐ _____
- ☐ _____

Notes:_____

_____

_____

_____

TIME	APPOINTMENTS

HIGHLIGHT OF THE DAY

EXPENSES

Gas: _____

Meals: _____

Mileage: _____

Other: _____

_____

words of wisdom

"In the business world, the rearview mirror is always clearer than the windshield."
—**Warren Buffett**, business magnate and philanthropist

Sunday

Prospecting Tasks

☐ _____
☐ _____
☐ _____
☐ _____
☐ _____
☐ _____

Marketing Tasks

☐ _____
☐ _____
☐ _____
☐ _____
☐ _____
☐ _____

Notes: _____

_____

_____

_____

TIME	APPOINTMENTS

HIGHLIGHT OF THE DAY

EXPENSES

Gas: _____

Meals: _____

Mileage: _____

Other: _____

_____

Weekly Wrap-Up

GOALS:

☐ Met

☐ Exceeded

☐ Maybe Next Week

Highlight of the Week: _____

_____

_____

Prospecting Notes: _____

_____

_____

Marketing Notes: _____

_____

_____

Networking Notes: _____

_____

_____

Professional Development Notes: _____

_____

_____

THOUGHTS ABOUT THE WEEK

Week 23

Dates: _____

Goals: _____

Monday

Prospecting Tasks

- ☐ _____
- ☐ _____
- ☐ _____
- ☐ _____
- ☐ _____
- ☐ _____

Marketing Tasks

- ☐ _____
- ☐ _____
- ☐ _____
- ☐ _____
- ☐ _____
- ☐ _____

Notes:_____

_____

_____

_____

TIME	APPOINTMENTS

HIGHLIGHT OF THE DAY

EXPENSES

Gas: _____

Meals: _____

Mileage: _____

Other: _____

_____

technology tips

Regular blogging over web technology can help you attract consumers because it is a great way to build trust and brand recognition at the same time.

Tuesday

Prospecting Tasks

- [ ] _____
- [ ] _____
- [ ] _____
- [ ] _____
- [ ] _____
- [ ] _____

Marketing Tasks

- [ ] _____
- [ ] _____
- [ ] _____
- [ ] _____
- [ ] _____
- [ ] _____

Notes:_____

_____

_____

_____

TIME   **APPOINTMENTS**

HIGHLIGHT OF THE DAY

EXPENSES

Gas: _____

Meals: _____

Mileage: _____

Other: _____

_____

prospecting pointers

Asking questions will not only help you learn a prospect's needs, but it will help you to suggest the right real estate solutions.

Wednesday

Prospecting Tasks

☐ _____

☐ _____

☐ _____

☐ _____

☐ _____

☐ _____

Marketing Tasks

☐ _____

☐ _____

☐ _____

☐ _____

☐ _____

☐ _____

Notes: _____

_____

_____

_____

TIME   APPOINTMENTS

HIGHLIGHT OF THE DAY

EXPENSES

Gas: _____

Meals: _____

Mileage: _____

Other: _____

_____

Partner with local lenders so that you can leverage each other's personal and business relationships.

Thursday

Prospecting Tasks

- ☐ _____
- ☐ _____
- ☐ _____
- ☐ _____
- ☐ _____
- ☐ _____

Marketing Tasks

- ☐ _____
- ☐ _____
- ☐ _____
- ☐ _____
- ☐ _____
- ☐ _____

Notes: _____

_____

_____

_____

TIME   APPOINTMENTS

HIGHLIGHT OF THE DAY

EXPENSES

Gas: _____

Meals: _____

Mileage: _____

Other: _____

_____

Look through your address book or review contacts in your smartphone. Call three business contacts to discuss ways that you can work together in order to generate leads.

Friday

Prospecting Tasks

☐ _____
☐ _____
☐ _____
☐ _____
☐ _____
☐ _____

Marketing Tasks

☐ _____
☐ _____
☐ _____
☐ _____
☐ _____
☐ _____

Notes: _____
_____
_____
_____

TIME   APPOINTMENTS

HIGHLIGHT OF THE DAY

EXPENSES

Gas: _____
Meals: _____
Mileage: _____
Other: _____
_____

live and learn

Give leads and referrals whenever possible. The best networkers believe that what goes around, comes around. You need to genuinely want to help the people you meet.

Saturday

Prospecting Tasks

☐ _____
☐ _____
☐ _____
☐ _____
☐ _____
☐ _____

Marketing Tasks

☐ _____
☐ _____
☐ _____
☐ _____
☐ _____
☐ _____

Notes: _____
_____
_____
_____

TIME   APPOINTMENTS

HIGHLIGHT OF THE DAY

EXPENSES

Gas: _____

Meals: _____

Mileage: _____

Other: _____

_____

words of wisdom

Sunday

Prospecting Tasks

- ☐ _____
- ☐ _____
- ☐ _____
- ☐ _____
- ☐ _____
- ☐ _____

Marketing Tasks

- ☐ _____
- ☐ _____
- ☐ _____
- ☐ _____
- ☐ _____
- ☐ _____

Notes:_____
_____
_____
_____

TIME **APPOINTMENTS**

HIGHLIGHT OF THE DAY

EXPENSES

Gas: _____

Meals: _____

Mileage: _____

Other: _____

_____

Weekly Wrap-Up

GOALS:

- ☐ Met
- ☐ Exceeded
- ☐ Maybe Next Week

Highlight of the Week: _____

_____

_____

Prospecting Notes: _____

_____

_____

Marketing Notes: _____

_____

_____

Networking Notes: _____

_____

_____

Professional Development Notes: _____

_____

_____

THOUGHTS ABOUT THE WEEK

Week 24

Dates: _____

Goals: _____

Monday

Prospecting Tasks

- ☐ _____
- ☐ _____
- ☐ _____
- ☐ _____
- ☐ _____
- ☐ _____

Marketing Tasks

- ☐ _____
- ☐ _____
- ☐ _____
- ☐ _____
- ☐ _____
- ☐ _____

Notes: _____

_____

_____

_____

TIME	APPOINTMENTS

HIGHLIGHT OF THE DAY

EXPENSES

Gas: _____

Meals: _____

Mileage: _____

Other: _____

_____

Tuesday

Prospecting Tasks

- ☐ _____
- ☐ _____
- ☐ _____
- ☐ _____
- ☐ _____
- ☐ _____

Marketing Tasks

- ☐ _____
- ☐ _____
- ☐ _____
- ☐ _____
- ☐ _____
- ☐ _____

Notes: _____
_____
_____
_____

TIME   **APPOINTMENTS**

HIGHLIGHT OF THE DAY

EXPENSES

Gas: _____

Meals: _____

Mileage: _____

Other: _____

_____

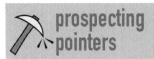

prospecting pointers

Instead of merely holding routine conversations, see how you can think differently and uniquely so that you can beat the monotony while marketing prospects.

Wednesday

Prospecting Tasks

- ☐ _____
- ☐ _____
- ☐ _____
- ☐ _____
- ☐ _____
- ☐ _____

Marketing Tasks

- ☐ _____
- ☐ _____
- ☐ _____
- ☐ _____
- ☐ _____
- ☐ _____

Notes:_____
_____
_____
_____

TIME   APPOINTMENTS

HIGHLIGHT OF THE DAY

EXPENSES

Gas: _____

Meals: _____

Mileage: _____

Other: _____

_____

 **marketing matters**

Use the power of emails with clear and concise content to create top of mind awareness with buyers and sellers. Prepare unique campaigns based on different target markets.

Thursday

Prospecting Tasks

- ☐ _____
- ☐ _____
- ☐ _____
- ☐ _____
- ☐ _____
- ☐ _____

Marketing Tasks

- ☐ _____
- ☐ _____
- ☐ _____
- ☐ _____
- ☐ _____
- ☐ _____

Notes:_____
_____
_____
_____

TIME   APPOINTMENTS

HIGHLIGHT OF THE DAY

EXPENSES

Gas: _____

Meals: _____

Mileage: _____

Other: _____

_____

A proper voice mail greeting can make a positive impression on your caller. Listen to your personal greeting and record a new one, if necessary.

Friday

Prospecting Tasks

☐ _____
☐ _____
☐ _____
☐ _____
☐ _____
☐ _____

Marketing Tasks

☐ _____
☐ _____
☐ _____
☐ _____
☐ _____
☐ _____

Notes:_____
_____
_____
_____

TIME   APPOINTMENTS

HIGHLIGHT OF THE DAY

EXPENSES

Gas: _____

Meals: _____

Mileage: _____

Other: _____

_____

 **live and learn**

Consider sponsoring various local events in order to increase your brand exposure and meet new contacts.

Saturday

Prospecting Tasks

☐ _____
☐ _____
☐ _____
☐ _____
☐ _____
☐ _____

Marketing Tasks

☐ _____
☐ _____
☐ _____
☐ _____
☐ _____
☐ _____

Notes:_____
_____
_____
_____

TIME	APPOINTMENTS

HIGHLIGHT OF THE DAY

EXPENSES

Gas: _____
Meals: _____
Mileage: _____
Other: _____
_____

"You fail your way to success. Successes are the failures that didn't quit."
—Gary Keller, author and co-founder of Keller Williams Realty.

Sunday

Prospecting Tasks

☐ _____
☐ _____
☐ _____
☐ _____
☐ _____
☐ _____

Marketing Tasks

☐ _____
☐ _____
☐ _____
☐ _____
☐ _____
☐ _____

Notes: _____
_____
_____
_____

TIME   APPOINTMENTS

HIGHLIGHT OF THE DAY

EXPENSES

Gas: _____
Meals: _____
Mileage: _____
Other: _____
_____

Weekly Wrap-Up

GOALS:

☐ Met

☐ Exceeded

☐ Maybe Next Week

Highlight of the Week: _____

_____

_____

Prospecting Notes: _____

_____

_____

Marketing Notes: _____

_____

_____

Networking Notes: _____

_____

_____

Professional Development Notes: _____

_____

_____

THOUGHTS ABOUT THE WEEK

Week 25

Dates: _____

Goals: _____

Monday

Prospecting Tasks

- ☐ _____
- ☐ _____
- ☐ _____
- ☐ _____
- ☐ _____
- ☐ _____

Marketing Tasks

- ☐ _____
- ☐ _____
- ☐ _____
- ☐ _____
- ☐ _____
- ☐ _____

Notes: _____

_____

_____

_____

TIME	APPOINTMENTS

HIGHLIGHT OF THE DAY

EXPENSES

Gas: _____

Meals: _____

Mileage: _____

Other: _____

_____

Tuesday

Prospecting Tasks

- ☐ _____
- ☐ _____
- ☐ _____
- ☐ _____
- ☐ _____
- ☐ _____

Marketing Tasks

- ☐ _____
- ☐ _____
- ☐ _____
- ☐ _____
- ☐ _____
- ☐ _____

Notes: _____

_____

_____

_____

TIME	APPOINTMENTS

HIGHLIGHT OF THE DAY

EXPENSES

Gas: _____

Meals: _____

Mileage: _____

Other: _____

_____

prospecting pointers

Get to know the needs and desires of your prospects and offer customized solutions that suit their needs and budget.

Wednesday

Prospecting Tasks

☐ _____
☐ _____
☐ _____
☐ _____
☐ _____
☐ _____

Marketing Tasks

☐ _____
☐ _____
☐ _____
☐ _____
☐ _____
☐ _____

Notes:_____

_____

_____

_____

TIME   APPOINTMENTS

HIGHLIGHT OF THE DAY

EXPENSES

Gas: _____

Meals: _____

Mileage: _____

Other: _____

_____

marketing matters

Consider the benefits of postcards in your direct mail campaign. Since a postcard is not in an envelope, its message will be seen— even if only for a split second.

Thursday

Prospecting Tasks

☐ _____
☐ _____
☐ _____
☐ _____
☐ _____
☐ _____

Marketing Tasks

☐ _____
☐ _____
☐ _____
☐ _____
☐ _____
☐ _____

Notes:_____
_____
_____
_____

TIME   APPOINTMENTS

HIGHLIGHT OF THE DAY

EXPENSES

Gas: _____

Meals: _____

Mileage: _____

Other: _____

_____

In order to generate some goodwill, coordinate a garage sale or canned food drive in your neighborhood farm area.

Friday

Prospecting Tasks

- ☐ _____
- ☐ _____
- ☐ _____
- ☐ _____
- ☐ _____
- ☐ _____

Marketing Tasks

- ☐ _____
- ☐ _____
- ☐ _____
- ☐ _____
- ☐ _____
- ☐ _____

Notes:_____

_____

_____

_____

TIME   APPOINTMENTS

HIGHLIGHT OF THE DAY

EXPENSES

Gas: _____

Meals: _____

Mileage: _____

Other: _____

_____

live and learn

The Internet is a great equalizer. Small businesses that effectively use the Internet can have a wider impact than their larger competitors. Seek opportunities to learn more about this invaluable resource.

Saturday

Prospecting Tasks

☐ _____
☐ _____
☐ _____
☐ _____
☐ _____
☐ _____

Marketing Tasks

☐ _____
☐ _____
☐ _____
☐ _____
☐ _____
☐ _____

Notes: _____
_____
_____
_____

TIME   APPOINTMENTS

HIGHLIGHT OF THE DAY

EXPENSES

Gas: _____
Meals: _____
Mileage: _____
Other: _____
_____

words of wisdom "The question isn't who is going to let me; it's who is going to stop me."
—Ayn Rand, Russian-born American
novelist, essayist, and philosopher

Sunday

Prospecting Tasks

- ☐ _____
- ☐ _____
- ☐ _____
- ☐ _____
- ☐ _____
- ☐ _____

Marketing Tasks

- ☐ _____
- ☐ _____
- ☐ _____
- ☐ _____
- ☐ _____
- ☐ _____

Notes:_____

_____

_____

_____

TIME	APPOINTMENTS

HIGHLIGHT OF THE DAY

EXPENSES

Gas: _____

Meals: _____

Mileage: _____

Other: _____

_____

Weekly Wrap-Up

GOALS:

☐ Met

☐ Exceeded

☐ Maybe Next Week

Highlight of the Week: _____ _____

_____

_____

Prospecting Notes: _____

_____

_____

Marketing Notes: _____

_____

_____

Networking Notes: _____

_____

_____

Professional Development Notes: _____

_____

_____

THOUGHTS ABOUT THE WEEK

Week 26

Dates: _____

Goals: _____

Monday

Prospecting Tasks

- ☐ _____
- ☐ _____
- ☐ _____
- ☐ _____
- ☐ _____
- ☐ _____

Marketing Tasks

- ☐ _____
- ☐ _____
- ☐ _____
- ☐ _____
- ☐ _____
- ☐ _____

Notes: _____

_____

_____

_____

TIME	APPOINTMENTS

HIGHLIGHT OF THE DAY

EXPENSES

Gas: _____

Meals: _____

Mileage: _____

Other: _____

_____

technology tips

When creating a business-related website, acquiring maximum domains matching the company's name and business can be a value addition.

Tuesday

Prospecting Tasks

- [ ] _____
- [ ] _____
- [ ] _____
- [ ] _____
- [ ] _____
- [ ] _____

Marketing Tasks

- [ ] _____
- [ ] _____
- [ ] _____
- [ ] _____
- [ ] _____
- [ ] _____

Notes:_____
_____
_____
_____

TIME	APPOINTMENTS

HIGHLIGHT OF THE DAY

EXPENSES

Gas: _____

Meals: _____

Mileage: _____

Other: _____

_____

Wednesday

Prospecting Tasks

☐ _____
☐ _____
☐ _____
☐ _____
☐ _____
☐ _____

Marketing Tasks

☐ _____
☐ _____
☐ _____
☐ _____
☐ _____
☐ _____

Notes:_____

_____

_____

_____

TIME   APPOINTMENTS

HIGHLIGHT OF THE DAY

EXPENSES

Gas: _____

Meals: _____

Mileage: _____

Other: _____

_____

marketing matters

Sponsor community events that benefit local organizations and also aid in advertising your real estate services.

Thursday

Prospecting Tasks

- ☐ _____
- ☐ _____
- ☐ _____
- ☐ _____
- ☐ _____
- ☐ _____

Marketing Tasks

- ☐ _____
- ☐ _____
- ☐ _____
- ☐ _____
- ☐ _____
- ☐ _____

Notes: _____

_____

_____

_____

TIME   **APPOINTMENTS**

HIGHLIGHT OF THE DAY

EXPENSES

Gas: _____

Meals: _____

Mileage: _____

Other: _____

_____

Prepare a mailing for your past clients or your circle of influence. Include valuable information, such as real estate tips and news, or an occasional marketing calendar or gift.

Friday

Prospecting Tasks

☐ _____
☐ _____
☐ _____
☐ _____
☐ _____
☐ _____

Marketing Tasks

☐ _____
☐ _____
☐ _____
☐ _____
☐ _____
☐ _____

Notes:_____
_____
_____
_____

TIME   APPOINTMENTS

HIGHLIGHT OF THE DAY

EXPENSES

Gas: _____
Meals: _____
Mileage: _____
Other: _____
_____

 **live and learn**

Establish a profile on an online business-networking portal, such as LinkedIn, to better connect with highly resourceful contacts and highlight your services.

Saturday

Prospecting Tasks

- ☐ _____
- ☐ _____
- ☐ _____
- ☐ _____
- ☐ _____
- ☐ _____

Marketing Tasks

- ☐ _____
- ☐ _____
- ☐ _____
- ☐ _____
- ☐ _____
- ☐ _____

Notes: _____

_____

_____

_____

TIME   APPOINTMENTS

HIGHLIGHT OF THE DAY

EXPENSES

Gas: _____

Meals: _____

Mileage: _____

Other: _____

_____

words of wisdom

"There are no secrets to success. It is the result of preparation, hard work, learning from failure."
—Colin Powell, American statesman and retired four-star general of the United States Army

Sunday

Prospecting Tasks

- ☐ _____
- ☐ _____
- ☐ _____
- ☐ _____
- ☐ _____
- ☐ _____

Marketing Tasks

- ☐ _____
- ☐ _____
- ☐ _____
- ☐ _____
- ☐ _____
- ☐ _____

Notes:_____
_____
_____
_____

TIME   APPOINTMENTS

HIGHLIGHT OF THE DAY

EXPENSES

Gas: _____

Meals: _____

Mileage: _____

Other: _____

_____

Weekly Wrap-Up

GOALS:

- ☐ Met
- ☐ Exceeded
- ☐ Maybe Next Week

Highlight of the Week: _____

_____

_____

Prospecting Notes: _____

_____

_____

Marketing Notes: _____

_____

_____

Networking Notes: _____

_____

_____

Professional Development Notes: _____

_____

_____

THOUGHTS ABOUT THE WEEK

CHART YOUR COURSE TO SUCCESS

The following tools will assist you as you chart your path to success in the field of real estate. Remember that there is something magical that goes on in your subconscious mind when you document your goals. And, when you document them in a place where you can continually look back and reflect on your personal accomplishments, you begin to exude success and a sense of achievement.

Have a look at the success tools included on the following pages:

Setting Your Income Goals. Using the chart provided, calculate the number of transactions needed to meet your financial goals for the next six months. Drill down to figure out the number of closings needed per month in order to achieve those goals.

Monthly Self-Assessment. The Weekly Wrap-Ups throughout the planner will help you to evaluate your weekly progress, and this chart will allow you to make long-term assessments. Be honest with yourself. In school and in life, nobody gets straight A's all the time. Any progress, no matter how small, should be praised.

Prospecting Planner. There's a big difference between prospecting and marketing. Learn the differences between the two. Then, calculate how many prospects you need to contact every year, month, week, and day in order to meet your goals.

Marketing Planner. Use the handy list of marketing activities and the sample marketing calendar to establish your own six-month marketing plan.

Working as a real estate agent is a very rewarding career choice. But, despite what those around you may believe, it is not easy. There are so many different components necessary to real estate success that a real estate agent is always juggling. Remember that when a juggler drops a ball, he picks it up and keeps on going. With real estate, you need to be that juggler. Just because one day or one week is particularly challenging, it doesn't mean that the next one will be. When you work through this planner and are consistent in your efforts, you will be pleased with the success that you can achieve.

Setting Your Income Goals

Calculate Number of Closings Needed

Step 1: *Calculate Average Commission per Closing*

Average sale price per property $_____

x _____ % commission due office

= total gross commission due office $_____

x _____ % commission split

= average commission per closing $_____

Step 2: *Calculate Closings Needed per Month*

Your annual income goal $_____

÷ average commission per closing $_____

= closings needed per year $_____

÷ 12

= closings needed per month $_____

Example

Step 1: *Calculate Average Commission per Closing*

Average sale price per property $250,000

x _3%_ commission due office

= total gross commission due office $7500

x _70%_ commission split

= average commission per closing $5250

Step 2: *Calculate Closings Needed per Month*

Your annual income goal $100,000

÷ average commission per closing $5250

= closings needed per year   19

÷ 12

= closings needed per month   1.58

Self-Assessment

Use the chart below to measure your progress and assess how well you have met your goals. The chart includes goals traditionally set by many real estate agents. Add your own numbers to the blank lines in the pre-written goals. You can also customize the chart and add your own goals in the space provided.

At the end of every month, assess your progress in each area by assigning yourself a score between 1 and 5. Did you get lots of high marks? If so, it's time to challenge yourself and set new goals for the next six months.

	Month 1	Month 2	Month 3	Month 4	Month 5	Month 6
Follow up on all leads on the day they were received.						
Email new listings to buyer prospects daily.						
Email ____ newsletters per month.						
Make _____ personal phone calls to circle of influence per month.						
Post to social media ____ times weekly.						
Send ____ postcards per month.						
Hold _____ open houses per month.						
Contact _____ FSBO/Expired/ Pre-foreclosure prospects per month.						

Prospecting

Lead generation falls into two categories: prospecting and marketing. You are prospecting when you actively obtain the leads yourself. You are marketing when you do things that make the leads come to you. It's *you* making contact with people as opposed to *people* making contact with you.

The information below will provide you with some ideas for prospecting activities that you can employ to generate leads. The handy chart will assist you to calculate the number of prospects needed to achieve your goals.

Sample Prospecting Activities

Face-to-Face
- Door-to-Door Neighborhood Canvasing
- Open Houses
- Networking Events
- Community Outreach
- Social Functions
- Educational Opportunities
- Booths at Events
- Past Client Pop-bys

Telemarketing
- For Sale By Owners / Expired Listings
- Notices of Default (Pre-foreclosure)
- Rental Community
- Past Clients
- Geographic Farm
- Banks
- Referral Sources

Calculate Number of Prospects Needed

Calculate the number of prospects needed per year
Total closings you want per year   _____
x 25 (prospect-to-sale ratio is 25 to 1)   _____
= total number of prospects needed   _____

Total number of prospects needed daily
Annual prospects needed   _____
÷ 12 months   _____
÷ 30 days   _____
= prospects needed per day   _____

Example

Calculate Number of Prospects Needed

Calculate the number of prospects needed per year
Total closings you want per year   _____20_____
x 25 (prospect-to-sale ratio is 25 to 1)   _____500_____
= total number of prospects needed   _____500_____

Total number of prospects needed daily
Annual prospects needed   _____500_____
÷ 12 months   _____41.6_____
÷ 30 days   _____1.38_____
= prospects needed per day   _____1-2_____

Marketing

Real estate marketing involves the things that you do in order to make the leads come to you. It's what you do to make the phone ring instead of you picking up the phone and making the call.

Use the information below in order to prepare a marketing calendar. Review the list of Sample Marketing Activities, and the sample marketing plan. Create a plan like the one on the next page. Include marketing activities that you enjoy. When you prepare a marketing plan, you chart a navigable course to success.

Sample Marketing Activities

Advertising
- Newspaper
- Radio
- Magazines
- Bus Stop Benches
- Shopping Carts
- Billboards
- Television
- Moving Vans

Promotional Items
- Magnets
- Calendars
- Note Pads
- Pens

Social Media
- Facebook
- Twitter
- Pinterest
- YouTube
- Google+

Direct Mail
- Postcard Campaigns
- Just Listed/Just Sold Cards
- Real Estate Market Updates
- Community Newsletters

Sponsorship
- Sports Teams
- Community Events
- Charity Events

Online Lead Generation Tools/Companies

Websites and Blogs

Voice Broadcast

Press Releases

Sample Marketing Plan

DECEMBER	JANUARY	FEBRUARY
■ Send non-denominational holiday cards to circle of influence	■ Send market information to geographic farm	■ Send tax tips newsletter to geographic farm and circle of influence
■ Post to social media sites daily	■ Send monthly newsletter to circle of influence	■ Post to social media sites daily
■ Write one blog post per week	■ Post to social media sites daily	■ Write one blog post per week
■ Post to Craigslist twice weekly	■ Write one blog post per week	■ Post to Craigslist twice weekly
	■ Post to Craigslist twice weekly	
	■ Clean up database	
	■ Call all contacts to wish them a Happy New Year and collect fresh email addresses	

GOALS for the next 6 months*

OVERALL GOALS
Earnings: _____

Deals Closed: _____

PROSPECTING GOALS
Starting Point: _____

_____

Goals: _____

_____

MARKETING GOALS
Starting Point: _____

_____

Goals: _____

_____

NETWORKING GOALS
Starting Point: _____

_____

Goals: _____

_____

PROFESSIONAL DEVELOPMENT GOALS
Starting Point: _____

_____

Goals: _____

_____

	NUMBER OF CLOSINGS	AVERAGE COMMISSION PER CLOSING
Last 6 Months		
Goal for Next 6 Months		

*To view a sample chart, see the Setting Goals section of this book. For assistance in calculating income or establishing marketing and prospecting plans, see pages 229–235.

236

Six-Month Wrap-Up

Congratulations! You've diligently completed six months of structured business planning and goal setting. Before you start your next planner, take a moment to reflect on your accomplishments over the last six months. Did you meet your goals? Jotting down a few thoughts about your achievements over the past six months will help you to set new goals for continued success in the field of real estate.

OVERALL GOALS

_____

_____

_____

PROSPECTING GOALS

_____

_____

MARKETING GOALS

_____

_____

NETWORKING GOALS

_____

_____

PROFESSIONAL DEVELOPMENT GOALS

_____

_____

Final Thoughts
What was your biggest source of closed transactions? How can you alter your future business plan to maximize your work with this lead source? Consider this as you begin to set new goals for the next six months.

Notes

Made in the USA
Lexington, KY
10 January 2014